SURFING PAYMENT CHANNELS—
MASTERING THE FRAUD TSUNAMI

SURFING PAYMENT CHANNELS

MASTERING THE FRAUD TSUNAMI

James D. Pitts

CONTENTS

The individual views expressed in this book do not necessarily reflect the views of the author, other contributing individuals, sponsoring organizations, the Financial Services Roundtable, FSTC, BITS or any of their member organizations.

In God We Trust

This book is dedicated to God, high-integrity financial institutions and governments, and all of the individual heroes who work relentlessly to fight payments fraud. Without trust and integrity a payment system will fail. The good health of payments systems enables productive commerce, makes strong economies possible, and allows for a high quality of life within organized societies.

I recently noticed a full page in a magazine touting two paragraphs and a three-quarter-page graphic that provided the results of a recent study done by the University of Hertfordshire. The study indicated that 88 percent of lost wallets with baby pictures get returned. The same exercise including pictures of dogs (53%) or older couples (28%) were significantly less effective. The results of the study appear to say that baby pictures help *most* honest people remember to be honest. The promotional nature of the article seemed to imply that you should carry pictures of babies (yours or otherwise) to deter theft. I guess carrying pictures of babies who aren't yours could be considered a publicly sanctioned fraudulent countermeasure to prevent the erosion of honesty—a lie to promote honesty, so to speak. When did life get so complicated?

This book is concerned with the harsh reality of thieves, not just situational ethics.

Fraudsters are thieves who will steal your wallet, your cash, your debit and credit cards, your personal identity, and any data they can glean from account or payment cards. They will also steal your baby's pictures in hopes of finding names, birthdates, and maybe social security numbers written on the backs of the photos so they can steal your baby's identity as well. They have no polite conscience or ethics, and they are enjoying great wealth—coming out of your wallet.

The Fraud Tsunami isn't coming. It's here!

Read on.

RICH OLIVER, FEDERAL RESERVE BANK OF ATLANTA

I have had the good fortune to have spent great portions of the last thirty-six years working in the payments industry as the payments system has slowly morphed itself from a predominantly paper-based mechanism to an electronic one. Throughout that period, I have closely watched and frequently had to address issues related to risk and fraud. As I look back, I have come to appreciate the simplicity of dealing with fraud in the less complex world of paper. Wrestling with check or cash counterfeiting, investigating a case of inside doctoring of payroll files, or chasing down an occasional instance of credit card fraud now seems, in retrospect, like a trivial exercise given the emergence of today's sophisticated attacks in the world of electronics. Education and awareness efforts in the 1980s involved such activities as listening to Frank Abagnale Jr., later played by Leonardo DiCaprio in *Catch Me If You Can*, talk about how he passed bad checks as part of his daring impersonation and fraud schemes. This was clearly the age of innocence that has now changed in the twenty-first century to an era of uneasiness.

For that matter, the changes have been so significant over time that the word "fraud" doesn't seem to adequately capture all the dimensions of today's environment. On a whim, I looked up fraud in the dictionary and found a very succinct definition, "Deception deliberately practiced; trickery." The breadth and depth of today's experience regarding fraud in the payments world seems far greater than anything implied by Webster. For that matter, I view "trickery" as a double reverse on the football field, not a global, Internet-based, complex account take-over and ID theft scheme in the payments world.

So what has happened to change the world of payments fraud to such an alarming degree? I would suggest five driving factors:

- Payments technology and the explosive growth of the Internet have magnified the possibilities of fraud far more than even the most pessimistic payments professional could imagine. While electronification has dramatically increased payments efficiency and even created the potential for more sophisticated risk controls, it has also created greater vulnerabilities for technology-savvy fraudsters to commit their crimes. A whole new vocabulary has arisen to warn us of Trojan horses, ZBOTS, malware, and phishing and pharming schemes. We hear of denial-of-service attacks on the daily news. "Identity theft" had to be a finalist for new phrase of the year in 2008. In response, we have implemented firewalls, created forensic programs, and blocked spam.

- Globalization is an outgrowth of our worldwide, industrial economic village. However, when coupled with the emergence of the Internet, it has greatly expanded the resource pool of fraudsters and facilitated their access to critical or sensitive systems around the world. The emergence of fraudulent activity centers in Western Africa, Eastern Europe, and the Far East has almost become a part of the fabric of global payments systems today.

- Criminal organizations have sprung up on a worldwide basis, creating their own Web sites and using publicly available online career management services to recruit talented individuals into their web. These organizations have the benefit of being virtual in nature, eliminating the concept of a physical presence as a point of focus for law enforcement. In many cases, principal players have never met face-to-face, further complicating law enforcement efforts. Yet, these shadowy organizations seem to have hierarchies, relationships, and duties/responsibilities common to any global business.

- Worldwide economic conditions have predictably expanded the number of individuals who see fraud and crime as a quick and easy way to make money. Unemployment is a powerful motivator that has created pools of so-called money mules willing to do the groundwork for global crime networks, accepting deposited funds, extracting their fee, and wiring the proceeds on to global concentration accounts.

- The state of today's worldwide media presence not only makes us more aware of existing payments fraud experiences, but also creates a wonderful reference library for aspiring criminals to copy. The concept of copycat crime has emerged in other criminal fields. White-collar crime areas, such as payments fraud, are no exception.

In the midst of this reality, it is natural to ask what can be done to address the growing problems of payments fraud. Unchecked by aggressive attention, what may be seen as ripples on a local payments pond can swell to become a tsunami of problems across the global oceans of payments systems. Solutions to the problems we collectively face will inevitably require greater levels of cooperation between payments providers, financial institutions, regulators, and law enforcement officials, a daunting challenge to say the least. But as a place to start, there is no better place than education and awareness. This book is an attempt to contribute to the education and awareness goal by sharing the thoughts of highly engaged industry professionals on a variety of payments fraud–related topics. In so doing, it should serve as a possible reference point for those ultimately charged with moving the ball forward to ensure that today's payments systems are prepared to survive the tsunami and continue to evoke public confidence.

CHAPTER ONE

COLLABORATING TO FIGHT PAYMENTS FRAUD

JAMES D. PITTS, FINANCIAL SERVICES TECHNOLOGY CONSORTIUM

FROM the very beginning of money as we know it, all transactions involving the exchange of something of value for something representing value have included a built-in risk for the payee or recipient of the payment. Nevertheless, money-based payments continue to flourish as they facilitate convenient commerce.

Early on things were simple enough. When a medieval farmer accepted a nobleman's letter in exchange for a pig, he was likely given silver or other coinage at a later date and may have been able to use the letter to acquire credit in the interim. He was happy to have been spared the tedium and risk associated with bartering the pig successfully otherwise. When the noble was not so noble and failed to make good on his promise of payment, the farmer may have had recourse through an organized legal system. Of course, the noble may have also been the sole available authority, so the farmer and his creditors may have simply lost out.

In China paper money was invented and introduced around 960 AD following a metal shortage. Without adequate supply of gold, silver and copper, the demand for coins could not be met. The construction of the great wall was financed by printing paper money. The oldest notes still in existence are from around 1400 AD. They bear a warning that anyone attempting to produce a copy of the note will be executed. So even with this ancient creation of a new payment method there was a significant understanding to protect it against fraudulent exploitation. There is evidence of earlier, cruder forms of paper money, but it was not widely accepted. It is highly likely that without the initial capitol deterrent, paper money may have never taken root.

In 1729 Benjamin Franklin made a convincing argument for paper money in his pamphlet, "A Modest Inquiry into the Nature and Necessity of a Paper Currency." Franklin makes winning arguments for the positive impact on the economy (versus precious metal coinage and bartering options) and the ability to manage the value of paper notes.

The learning curve associated with paper payments and fraud over the years since has had many ups and downs. The payments fraud game of cat and mouse continues today with U.S. paper money. Security threads, color-shifting ink, and watermarks are just a few of the countermeasures employed to keep our money safe. Of course it's not just about paper risks anymore. As the world evolves, transactions with their associated risks continue to become more complicated from many perspectives.

It seems like only yesterday when I walked into a salon for a haircut and the clerk asked me for several bits of personal information, including my social security number. This was pretty typical back then as people began to realize the value of collecting customer information. About that same time banks were happily accommodating the printing of state driver's license numbers as well as social security numbers on checks to streamline check approvals with retailers. Since then the United States Post Office has teamed up with the Federal Trade Commission to fight identity theft while happily admitting that only 2 percent of identity theft victims were reporting that the theft of their identity was connected to the mail. I'm guessing that even Al Gore never thought people would be silly enough to use credit cards over the internet back when he and those other folks invented it.

My earliest personal experience with payments fraud that I'm aware of was when a restaurant employee treated some friends to a party by imprinting a second ticket with my credit card while closing out my purchase. I ended up getting reimbursed, plus I got a fifty-dollar gift certificate as an apology. I thought, "Wow being a fraud victim is cool." I've been hit a couple of times since then with numbers in the hundreds and even thousands, but I've always been kept whole by "the powers that be."

Recently my innocent baby daughter (Okay, she's an adult—and now probably ticked off at me.) was attacked to the tune of thousands. She was very upset needless to say, but her bank kept her from actual harm. Okay, so my advice to her is to shred everything, don't give out personal information, never click on links in unsolicited e-mails, don't use obvious passwords and change them regularly, check your credit report, and keep duct tape on hand in case of chemical attack. Meanwhile, I'm thinking, "Thank God that honest people and high integrity institutions do so much to protect the rest of us from fraudulent payment transactions.

In modern times, trust in God, banks, and governments has allowed paper money to gain pretty much universal acceptance in spite of the ever-present risks. Hence the expression: "In God we trust. All others pay cash." Institutionalized trust in paper money has morphed into the many types of payments and transactions being embraced in today's financial world. Transactions in the form of paper, and even invisible data promises to pay, have grown exponentially. Unfortunately, theft by fraud has proliferated greatly as well. It seems criminals can be equally trusted to effectively attack each new payment channel with multiple fraud methodologies. Of course, mitigation by gallows or axe is no longer in the good guys' solution portfolio. Instead we face the ever-increasing demand for more sophisticated, compliant, and effective countermeasures to maintain acceptable risk levels within this ever-expanding battlefield.

Notice I didn't say "eliminate the risk." A nice thought, but will it ever be practical? There is an expression among the group of professionals who are considered to be payments security experts. "The only perfectly secure transaction is a transaction so secure that it cannot be completed." Never-the-less the "holy grail" in this realm continues to be "a perfectly secure transaction," and is much sought after through endless discussion, analytics, research, and invention.

Certainly we can agree that "trust in the system" has allowed development of many alternative payment types, channels, and transaction accounts - mostly fueled by consumer demand for convenience. This is truly a good thing for commerce. The facilitation of consumer or business payment capabilities any time, any where, and any way for anyone and anything is good. However, exponential payment alternatives equal exponential fraud alternatives equal exponential countermeasures requirements. Complex, constantly changing technology makes constant innovation and adaptation of countermeasures essential.

The financial equation in the war on payments fraud is more than slightly in favor of the bad guys, making the war even more of an uphill battle for us good guys. Think about it. Every dollar a fraudster gains is potential profit. He or she can spend 80 cents to steal that dollar and still make a handy 20 percent profit. A financial service provider supplying payments capabilities to businesses might get paid a nickel for the service, expecting to net a penny for a 20 percent profit. The business may have 80 cents of costs associated with that dollar of income in order to make a 20 percent margin. How much can the payment service provider and the business owner spend to avoid that fraud? Certainly not as much as the perpetrator can spend to fulfill the crime.

DON'T WORRY. CRIME DOESN'T PAY!

According to the U.S. Department of Justice:

- Only 15 percent of fraud victims report their losses to authorities
- Monetary losses from fraud exceeds $40 billion annually
- The prison population is taking a toll on some state budgets
- The average time spent in state prisons for first offense fraud convictions in 1999 was 1.58 years
- The average time spent in state prisons for second offense fraud convictions in 1999 was 1.16 years
- 1/3 of individuals interviewed experienced fraud attacks within the prior 12 months

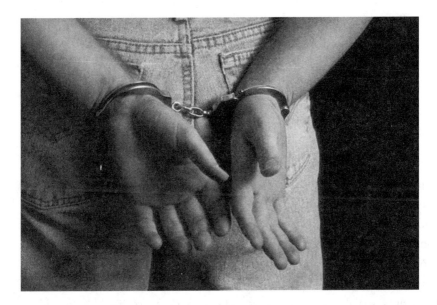

The man wearing handcuffs in this photo was a model who was fairly compensated for his time spent on the photo shoot. No actual criminals were made to feel restricted or uncomfortable in any way.

Quote from an internet fraud attorney's web site:

If the search and seizure of your property was done illegally, we may be able to keep evidence that could potentially be used against you out of court.

Did I mention that crime doesn't pay?

Typical cyber fraudster profile:

A twenty-something, eastern European with a seven figure income who goes to lunch in a black luxury car accompanied by a second black luxury car that is occupied by his or her body guards.

It's not just a "foreign problem." According to the U.S. department of justice, over 70 percent of internet-related crimes are home-based in the United States. A study done by Symantec Corporation indicates 46 percent of underground servers are in the United States.

The overhead associated with online-payments-related fraud is notable.

A study done (also by Symantec Corporation) detailed the following price ranges.

Bank account credentials: $10 to $1000
Credit cards with CVV2 numbers: $0.50 to $12

Credit cards: $0.10 to $25
E-mail addresses: $0.30/MB to $40/MB
E-mail passwords: $4 to $30
Full identities: $0.90 to $25
Cash-out services: 8 percent to 50 percent of total value
Scams: $2.50 to $100/week for hosting; $5 to$20 for design

When you come to fully appreciate the criminal's ability to adapt and innovate, especially utilizing www related capabilities, you may find yourself struggling not to succumb to a pressing sense of futility. If you think about the statistics you may even find your "trust factor" trying to slide around a bit. But it's comforting to know that for the tens of thousands of malicious viruses skulking about the web—you can purchase anti virus technology to protect yourself from hundreds of them. Isn't it? ... In God we trust, but protect your passwords, PINs, magstripes, social security numbers ... because *all* others should be considered to be suspected skimmers, hackers, spoofers, phishers, fraudsters ... and seriously scary digital boogie people!

Sorry, I got a little anxious there for a minute or two. Where was I? Okay.

In this rapidly evolving payment-fraud environment, it seems only logical that one effective preventative measure could be to improve the collaborative efforts and capabilities of the "good guys,", i.e. the financial services industry facilitating legitimate commerce. However, there are many collaboration gaps within financial institutions and the whole industry, and these gaps need to be addressed. The gaps appear to be perpetuated by stumbling blocks and priorities. Even so, there are some basic efforts we can make to better collaborate. Technology can make this collaboration much more effective if we can get past the traditional barriers.

Financial Industry Collaboration Gaps

- single client/multiple lines of business
- inter-institution sharing is informal/non-existent
- intra-institution sharing may be informal, very limited, or non-existent
- incident reporting lag can be days to months
- excessive manual requirements
- integration/inflexible legacy systems

- standardization of process
- measured service levels/reporting
- timely alerts/escalation

Financial Industry Collaboration Opportunities

- intra- and inter-institution emergency alerts
- improved incident reporting and tracking
- statistical data trends and analysis
- service level tracking and reporting
- industry trend reporting
- criminal activity warnings
- emerging technology and solutions
- best practices sharing

Beyond these basic issues within and between individual institutions, there exists an intuitive need to expand collaboration efforts to include law enforcement, retailers, corporations, and government organizations. Unfortunately there are even more barriers to solving the issues associated with generating this expansion of collaboration. These include legal and regulatory issues, conflicting drivers and priorities, and even the lack of a common vernacular and understanding of the full range of crime methodologies and countermeasures.

Of course the more basic approach to fighting payment fraud is *simply* to identify the different crimes being committed and techniques used and *just* develop and implement effective prevention countermeasures. Certainly, that's being done in many, many ways, but clearly there is nothing *simple* about it. The Financial Services Technology Consortium defined a high-level starting point in such an effort indicating over thirty payment types, product groups, and payment channels with over one hundred attack descriptions, each impacting a significant cross section of the defined areas. A quick calculation indicates thousands of potential known attack possibilities. Additionally, you have to consider that different attackers use differing methodologies, techniques, and tactics. To fully map out the entire spectrum you'd find we're not dealing with just hundreds of elements, but thousands or tens of thousands.

To reach back to my earlier analogy, this begs the question: Is it only one "holy grail" or will thousands be required to keep the faith or frankly, continue to assure the "trust"? If you're an operations guy like me, the grey matter is firing sparks at you such as legacy systems, integration issues, and always: What's the re$ource pain going to be? A likely response from an operational perspective might be, "Holy ... Grail!?!" (or something like that).

Fortunately, today we may find a few pure-hearted knights heroically delivering on the vision of the grail. This book includes perspectives from several who are fighting this good fight and winning against the great devil called payments fraud. Enjoy the literary sip from the grail provided herein and a promise of better knowledge you can use to strengthen your efforts to be successful in "Mastering the Fraud Tsunami."

This surf is certainly up! It is also deep, wide, and relentless. Grab your credit card, smart phone, PC, and maybe your water wings. Let's catch the wave!

CHAPTER TWO

CYBER CRIMES AGAINST FINANCIAL INSTITUTIONS AND THEIR CUSTOMERS

BILL NELSON, FS-ISAC

A S a banker in the 1980s, I was involved with developing and managing new electronic payment and information products. At the time, I had no inkling of how technology would eventually evolve and change the entire infrastructure of the payments system and the way services would ultimately be delivered to customers. An all-electronic Automated Clearing House (ACH) network, electronic draft data capture of card purchases, and the electronification of checks are just a few of the examples of important steps taken in the respective ACH, card, and check payment systems. These technology enhancements significantly reduced costs and associated operating and fraud risks with each of these payment systems.

In the last fifteen years, there has been a major trend toward putting banking enterprise systems and customer payment initiation capabilities on the World Wide Web. Convenience and cost reduction has been the driving force behind this trend, but it has presented a whole new set of security challenges and exposed a significant number of vulnerabilities within banking enterprise systems and customer payment services. The result has been an exponential increase in attacks from cyber criminals, insiders, and even nation states against financial institutions, payment processors, and end users of payment services.

The Cyber Crime Problem

How big is the problem? Verizon's Data Breach Investigations Study reports that there were over 285 million compromised records in the most recent year. Financial services continue to be the most targeted industry sector, growing to 93 percent of all attacks. The most recent Association for Financial Professionals (AFP) survey reported that 80 percent of the respondents had attempted or actual payments fraud directed at their companies. Law enforcement reports that 90 percent of these attacks were the result of organized criminal activities.

The Internet has enabled suppliers and users of cyber crime activities to link up. Some examples of these linkages are as follows:

- Online libraries and advertisements of stolen data
- Education on how to launch spamming, phishing, and keylogging attacks
- Advertisements for partners for complex fraud schemes
- Recruitment
- Detailed information sharing on technical vulnerabilities of software and specific financial institutions and their service providers
- Hacking services
- Keylogging and custom malware
- Spamming services
- How-to guides on defeating security and anti-fraud measures
- Open buying of information, stolen databases, demand deposit account (DDA) and card data, and so forth
- Renegade hosting
- Document forging
- Illegal pornography
- Form grabbers
- Spamming programs
- Money laundering services
- Phishing tool kits

The black market for this data enables the cyber criminal to purchase malware such as a Zeus credential-stealing Trojan for $1,200 or less. Other data, such as card numbers with PINs or the Card Verification Value (CVV or CVV2) security code, are also sold online with guarantees promised by the sellers if the cards do not work.

Vishing and Smishing

Two of the more common attacks seen against retail customers of financial institutions are vishing and smishing. Vishing is a type of phishing attack where the attacker gathers information under false pretenses for fraudulent purposes via Voice over Internet Protocol (VoIP). VoIP also allows caller ID spoofing, which means that the telephone number displayed on the recipient's caller ID is not the actual originating number. Vishing is difficult for law enforcement to trace. Here's how a typical vishing scheme works:

- The criminal configures an auto-dialer to call numbers in a given locale.
- The consumers receive an automated recording that alerts them that their credit card or DDA has fraudulent activity.
- The message instructs consumers to call a phone number that has a spoofed caller ID indicating a bank or credit union name.
- When the phone number is called, the consumers are given instructions to enter their credit/debit card numbers and CVV security code/ PIN on their keypads.
- Once the cyber criminal collects that information, then fraudulent cards are produced.

A spin-off of vishing is smishing and works much in the same way. Short Message Service (SMS) texting is used to deliver the bait to trick consumers to divulge personal information. An example is, "Your account has been suspended, call (999) 999-9999 immediately to reactivate." Or there is a link to an illegitimate Web site provided in the SMS text message. If the consumers call the phone number, an automated voice system or actual person instructs them to confirm their accounts by entering their credit or debit card numbers, CVV, PIN, or other personal information. That information is used to create fraudulent credit or debit cards.

Many of these cyber criminals are located in Eastern Europe or other countries that are outside the laws of the United States. The banks in their countries are aware of these schemes. If the cyber criminals try to issue the fraudulent cards there, then the local police may have them arrested. A less risky method to turn these fraudulent cards into cash is to employ money mules in other countries.

The Role of Money Mules

The cyber criminals often need money mules to move the funds out of the American banking system and back to their respective countries. The recruitment for these money mules may be as direct as an Internet advertisement for "financial fraud scheme, opportunity to make millions." Or, more recently, the cyber criminals have been more selective and gone onto reputable employment Web sites to selectively target individuals with an e-mail job offer such as this:

- Duties of the service representatives include holding and supporting a local business used for payments processing between the company and the clients
- Advanced user ability to operate computer and use Internet and e-mail
- An existing bank account opened on personal or business name
- Basic skills in managing payments and money transfers
- Availability of spare time (three to four hours per day)
- A basic salary of $2,500 monthly plus payments turnover bonus

These types of e-mail solicitations appear to some recipients to be legitimate offers and meet with a fairly high percentage of positive responses, particularly among the unemployed.

Once the money mules have been set up, the cyber criminal can use them for their particular scheme. One of the earliest schemes was in the carding environment where the cyber criminals would ship fraudulent gift, payroll, or ATM cards with PINs to the money mules and have them withdraw cash from local ATMs. The cash would then be shipped back to the cyber criminals with the money mules keeping 10 to 25 percent of the cash withdrawn. The most successful single carding scheme occurred in 2008 and consisted of a coordinated attack to withdraw $9 million in thirty minutes from one hundred and thirty ATMs in forty-nine countries. The attack masterminds fraudulently duplicated and upped withdrawal limits on payroll and gift cards issued by a large international bank.

Business Account Takeover

More recently, money mules have been used for sophisticated business account takeover schemes. Typically, these are targeted attacks against the finance officer or person within a small- to medium-sized business that the cyber criminal believes has online banking credentials. A spear phishing e-mail ("spear" because it is targeting one individual) is sent to the target, requesting he click an embedded link in the e-mail. The content of the e-mail suggests to the target that the e-mail is legitimate, such as a subpoena to appear in court, a Microsoft security update, a Better Business Bureau complaint, and so forth. However, when the target clicks the link, it takes him to a Web site that then places malware on his individual computer. The malware contains keylogging software that harvests the user's online banking credentials to then move money out of his business accounts. The cyber criminals typically use ACH credits to send the funds to multiple money mules throughout the United States, or they sometimes use Fedwire. The money mules then withdraw the funds in cash and send the money to the cyber criminals, usually in Eastern Europe via a Western Union MoneyGram or cash, keeping a percentage as their commission for this service.

How successful have these business account takeover schemes been? Examples of the losses include $700,000 from a school district, $1.2 million from a Texas company, and $100,000 from a electronics testing firm. The total attempted fraud and losses from these attacks is estimated at the hundreds of millions of dollars just in the last year.

There are several reasons for the success of these types of business account takeover attacks:

- The spear phishing e-mails are becoming more believable. The cyber criminals are constantly updating their templates used for these spear phishing attacks. Even if the target is aware of spear phishing schemes, he may fall prey for a believable template and click the embedded link.
- The cyber criminals have broken through online security procedures through sophisticated keylogging Trojans that have even compromised one-time passwords (OTPs.) Once the keylogging software is on the computer and network, the cyber criminal is receiving instant messages (IMs) of what the target is keying into his computer. So when the target keys in the user ID, password, and OTP, the cyber criminal can

be keying in the same information, stopping the target's computer from sending the legit messages to his bank and, in essence, hijacking the entire online banking session. The target may get a fake maintenance page, message telling him that the online banking session is temporarily down. Or another way to cover the tracks of a successful bank account takeover is for the hacker to install kill operating system (KOS), a $700 piece of malware that allows the hacker to shut down or prevent the infected machine from rebooting. Shutting down the machine allows the criminal to remove the victim's Internet access before the fraudulent funds transfers are realized and the attack can be mitigated.

- Many business users of online banking services and, in some cases, their banks have not taken these attacks seriously. They either have not heard of the attacks. If they have, they are often willing to risk the potential losses versus the convenience of their current procedures. The reality is that the current procedures are lacking in some of the most fundamental security best practices. Many companies believe that antivirus software will stop these types of attacks. However, it is difficult, if not impossible, for most antivirus software to detect these spear phishing attacks and their corresponding malware. The cyber criminals move their Web sites too frequently, and the antivirus software cannot keep up.

The Role of the FS-ISAC

The Financial Services Information Sharing and Analysis Center (FS-ISAC) provides the 24x7x365 platform for its members to share information between themselves, with the government and law enforcement, and with other sectors. The FS-ISAC was formed in 1999 in response to the 1998 Presidential Decision Directive 63 (PDD63) that called for the public and private sector to work together to address cyber threats to the nation's critical infrastructures. After September 11 and in response to Homeland Security Presidential Directive 7 (HSPD7) and the Homeland Security Act, the FS-ISAC expanded its role to encompass physical threats to our sector.

The FS-ISAC is a 501(c)6 nonprofit organization and is funded by its member firms and sponsors. In 2004, there were only sixty-eight members of the FS-ISAC, mostly larger financial services firms. Since that time, the membership has expanded to over forty-one hundred organizations, including commercial banks and credit unions of all sizes, brokerage firms, insurance companies, payments processors, and over forty trade associations representing the majority of the American financial services sector. The FS-ISAC works closely with various government agencies including the United States Department of Treasury, Department of Homeland Security, Federal Reserve, United States Secret Service, Federal Bureau of Investigation, National Security Agency, Central Intelligence Agency, and state and local governments.

The overall objective of the FS-ISAC is to protect the financial services sector against cyber and physical threats and risk. It acts as a trusted third party that provides anonymity to allow members to submit threat, vulnerability, and incident information in a non-attributable and trusted manner so information that would normally not be shared is able to be provided from the originator and shared for the good of the sector, the membership, and the nation. A partial list of FS-ISAC information sharing services and activities include:

- Provides timely, relevant, and actionable cyber and physical e-mail alerts from various sources distributed through the 24x7x365 FS-ISAC Security Operations Center (SOC)
- Prepares risk mitigation best practices and tool kits
- Sponsors subject matter expert (SME) committees including, the Threat Intelligence Committee and Business Resilience Committee that provide in-depth analyses of risks to the sector; provide technical, business, and operational impact assessments; and recommend mitigation and remediation strategies and tactics
- Hosts document repositories for members to share information and documentation with other members
- Provides an anonymous online submission capability to facilitate member sharing of threat, vulnerability, and incident information in a non-attributable and trusted manner
- Operates e-mail list servers supporting attributable information exchange by various special interest groups
- Facilitates anonymous surveys that allow members to request anonymized information regarding security best practices at other organizations
- Conducts biweekly threat information sharing calls for members to

discuss the latest threats, vulnerabilities, and incidents and allows guest
speakers on risk-related subjects

- Provides emergency threat or incident notifications to all members
  using the Critical Infrastructure Notification System (CINS)

A key factor in all of these activities is trust. The FS-ISAC works to facilitate
development of trust between its members and with other organizations in the
financial services sector, other sectors, and government organizations, particularly the law enforcement and intelligence communities.

The Importance of Public/Private Sector Information Sharing

Law enforcement and a number of government agencies have taken a lead
role working with the FS-ISAC, its member organizations, payments processors, and the financial services sector as a whole to combat these types of
attacks. An example of a successful instance of government/financial services
sector information sharing occurred on August 24, 2009, when the FBI; the
FS-ISAC; and National Automated Clearing House Association (NACHA), the
rule-making body for the Automated Clearing House network, released a joint
bulletin concerning account takeover activities targeting business and corporate
customers. The bulletin described the methods and tools employed in recent
fraud activities perpetrated against small- to medium-sized businesses that had
been reported to the FBI. The objective of the information sharing and ultimately the bulletin was to employ FS-ISAC and NACHA subject matter expertise
applied to the FBI case information to identify detailed threat detection and
risk mitigation strategies for financial institutions and their business customers,
while preserving the integrity of the FBI's ongoing investigations. The bulletin
was distributed through the FS-ISAC to its over forty-one hundred members,
which includes over forty member associations such as NACHA, the American
Bankers Association, Independent Community Bankers Association, amongst
others. It was also distributed separately through the Association for Financial
Professionals and recently through the United States Chamber of Commerce.

The FBI/FS-ISAC/NACHA joint bulletin detailed specific risk mitigation
recommendations regarding the business account takeover threat. They included:

- **Initiate ACH and wire transfer payments under dual control.** Some
  of the businesses that had been victims of the business account takeover

attacks reportedly did not have dual control for initiation and release of their online payments. Having that security procedure may have prevented losses in some of these cases.

- **Online commercial banking customers execute all online banking activities from a dedicated, locked-down computer system from where e-mail and Web browsing are not possible.** This recommendation, while it appears costly to some, is actually quite cost effective when considering the potential for loss if this procedure is not adopted. Frankly, the cost of a computer pales compare to the loss of $100,000, $1,000,000, or more, as have been reported from these attacks.

- **Limit administrative rights on users' workstations to prevent inadvertent downloading of malware.** Unfortunately, many small firms are not aware that this standard IT security recommendation exists. Giving full administrative rights to users' workstations is a recipe for major vulnerability exploits not just for business account takeover attacks, but also when it comes to various exploits of Microsoft, Adobe, and other software applications.

- **Reconcile all banking transactions on a daily basis.** Daily review of all business banking transactions is a sound cash management practice that helps identify fraudulent activity and can prevent losses from occurring.

- **Financial institutions should also implement an awareness communications program to advise customers of current threats and fraud activities.** Some financial institutions are holding online banking security forums for their business customers and reaching out to ensure that they are educated about the risks and mitigation tactics to employ to prevent losses.

- **Financial institutions implement appropriate fraud detection and mitigation best practices.** Transaction risk profiling helps banks identify anomalies in the payment activity of their customers. These anomalies should be reported to the business customers so they can identify potential fraudulent activity.

- **Financial institutions should consider using manual or automated out-of-band authentication systems.** In concert with fraud detection systems, examples of out-of-band authentication systems include manual client callback, automated SMS text messaging, and interactive voice response system callback to a known phone number with a PIN code. If the client's computer network is compromised, these out-of-band solutions help identify any attempted fraudulent payment activity and can prevent funds from being released.

The bulletin contained fourteen additional in-depth defenses that help shore up the security defenses of the financial institutions' enterprise and its customers' payment initiation practices.

Testing Enterprise and Customer Security

Another key component of improving the security posture of a financial institution or of its customers' payments processes is to test it periodically. A number of security firms and consultants offer vulnerability tests and ethical hacking tests, and organizations can take these effective preventive measures to protect against attacks. In the card payment arena, if retailers, financial institutions, or processors experience a breach, a qualified incident response assessor (QIRA) is brought in to assess the extent of the breach, eliminate the malware, and ensure that the vulnerabilities are addressed so future breaches do not occur.

Industry-wide exercises are another effective tool to build awareness, identify best practices, and improve the security of the entire financial services sector. The FS-ISAC has been at the forefront of supporting government exercises such as the Department of Homeland Security's Cyber Storm and the Financial Services Sector Coordinating Council's Cyberfire. More recently, the FS-ISAC launched the Cyber Attack against Payment Processes (CAPP) exercise that is more specific to retail payments including ACH, check, and card. The objectives of the CAPP exercise were to:

- Test the ability of financial institutions, processors, associations, and the industry to respond to major cyber attack incidents
- Raise awareness and educate financial services firms of all sizes regarding cyber threats to their enterprises, processors, and customers
- Make recommendations for improvements to cyber incident response procedures
- Evaluate and develop appropriate risk mitigation recommendations in response to the cyber payments attacks used in this exercise

- Engage participants going forward on the need to share threat, vulnerability, and incident information
- Develop an after-action report that can be used for workshops, webinars, and ongoing educational sessions regarding the lessons learned from the exercise

The CAPP Exercise Planning Committee was comprised of individuals with backgrounds in ACH, check, card processor, treasury management, and retailing. The attack vectors used in the exercise included spear phishing attacks with malware, denial-of-service attacks, point-of-sale (POS) device skimming, and internal fraud. The process involves a virtual survey tool and occurred over three days with daily injects and anonymous responses from the participants. As over seven hundred participants engaged in the 2010 CAPP exercise, the plan is to roll it out annually to continue to build awareness and improve the cyber security of the financial services industry and its customers.

What Does it All Mean?

Cyber criminals are continually finding ways to inject their malware onto machines by whatever means necessary. Custom malware will defeat antivirus security, and targeted attacks pose a significant problem for security vendors. These facts increase the reliance on the financial services industry to share information to protect themselves and their customers. I would urge all financial institutions and their customers to take steps to protect their payment processes. These include:

- Implement strong authentication and controls
- Improve network monitoring, fraud detection techniques, and overall IT security practices
- Perform risk assessments of IT software and hardware supply chain
- Educate your employees and customers
- Become an active participant in information sharing
- Understand, prepare, and react quickly to work on developing long-term infrastructure solutions

Information Sources
http://www.fsisac.com/
http://www.fsscc.com/
http://www.us-cert.gov/
http://www.fbi.gov/majcases/fraud/internetschemes.htm

CHAPTER THREE

CHANGING THE WAY THE WORLD COUNTS CASH

LARRY ROBINSON, ARMOR SAFE TECHNOLOGIES

I have spent my entire career working to solve cash management headaches. Over the years, I have learned that fraud is likely to occur wherever cash or cash equivalents is being handled. It can be carried out in wildly imaginative ways by colorful characters, but, more often, it occurs in perfectly mundane ways, perpetrated by relatively ordinary people who fail to resist the temptation to augment their personal income, tax-free no less, when they encounter what they believe to be an exploitable vulnerability in a cash management process. Keeping honest people honest is what good cash management process is all about.

My Childhood Home on the Line

In 1977, at twenty years of age, my wife Becky and I became 7-Eleven's youngest franchisees, buying a store in Nampa, Idaho. 7-Eleven is a great company, but they don't trust just any hardworking, poor kid from a remote mountain town with a franchise store. With my parent's home in the Rocky Mountains as the bank's collateral on our loan, Becky and I were extremely eager to pay off the loan as quickly as possible. Labor savings often makes the biggest difference to a company's bottom line, so Becky and I took turns working twelve hours on and twelve hours off, seven days a week through the first summer we owned the store. We often slept in the back of the store. We had one part-time employee, a close friend of ours, who helped during peak times. It wasn't long before 7-Eleven audited us for our conspicuously negligible labor costs, and we set division records for our store's profitability. We paid down our loan quickly and decided to hire additional help to work the grueling graveyard shift from eleven to seven.

A Good Christian Kid

At the time, Nampa was a sleepy farm community with a population of thirty-five thousand located west of Boise. Nampa is home to Northwest Nazarene College (NNC). We decided we would recruit the first employees for our 7-Eleven store almost exclusively from NNC. This seemed like a good idea because NNC was a Christian college after all.

On the new employee's second day, I was reconciling money order sales to the register and noticed that he had printed $650 more in money orders than he rang up with the money order key. Being new to retail and perhaps a little naïve, I assumed the clerk would be over $650 when we counted his deposits in the drop safe. Surely, he just forgot to ring up the money orders. We counted the cash, and he was not over. He had simply stolen the money orders. I called the clerk and gave him two options:

- He could come down to the store and meet with the police to explain the missing money orders.
- He could see to it that $650 in money orders miraculously showed up in my drop safe, along with his resignation letter, the next morning.

He went with the second option. While I'm not trying to disparage my fellow NNC students, I do want to emphasize that you cannot assume people are honest based on their background or credentials. Cash management procedures need to be in place that remove the temptation of easy money.

Nampa has a quaint downtown area with buildings built during the 1880s. One of our favorite places to eat lunch was a small café in a restored building. The owner used an antique register to ring up the sales. It was a beautiful, old cash register made by NCR. I noticed that, when this one particular waitress served us, she would open the register without ringing up our meal. I observed this a couple times and thought it seemed strange because every other waitress always rang the sale into this antique register. I called the owner and told him what we had observed. A month later, he called me back to thank me. Since he had let her go, his lunch sales had increased by over $100 per day, yet his purchases to his suppliers had not increased at all. In other words, the charming mother of two, our attentive waitress, was stealing $100 a day or more in cash sales.

Money Maker Systems

7-Eleven has a great franchise system and does a masterful job of teaching their franchisees how to run a rock-solid convenience store. If you look at the management teams of many of the convenience stores in the United States, you will often find 7-Eleven alumni. Part of 7-Eleven's system back in the 1970s was what they called shift analysis. The idea was to monitor sales on a given shift throughout each week and compare it to sales on the same shift for the last few months, looking for any trends that follow particular cashiers, such as a cashier who always exceeds or falls below the sales average on the same shift. Any cashier that falls below the average are either so rude that people avoid your store when the clerk is behind the counter or, more likely, the cashier is short-ringing his sales. For a pack of cigarettes that cost $1.05, a cashier might ring up the five cents and charge the customer $1.05. After doing this twenty times in a day, the cashier could simply put a twenty-dollar bill in his pocket and still balance his shift to the penny.

In 1985, Phil McRee, a fellow 7-Eleven franchisee, and I started a company called Money Maker Systems to automate the shift analysis system that 7-Eleven had taught us. We sold this system to fellow franchisees throughout Idaho, Oregon, California, and Nevada. We learned a lot from selling to our peers. One of our selling points was the time savings derived from automating the shift analysis process. Money Maker software was a precursor to backroom accounting systems used by retailers today, which are now very sophisticated and have further reduced labor and opportunities for fraud by interfacing with the POS systems.

Cash Manager

During a training session in California on the Money Maker software, a 7-Eleven franchisee said that our software did not save her as much time as we claimed. I sat in the back room with her and watched as she went through the process. I noticed that it took her only fifteen minutes to load the sales information into the software and up to an hour to count all of the money from the day. She had to take the money out of drop envelopes and compare it to a manual drop sheet. It was not only labor-intensive, but dangerous, as every employee that ever worked in her store knew she spent more than an hour a day in the back room with thousands of dollars out on her desk while she counted and made sense of the daily deposits.

It's good for a lot of obvious reasons that my first entrepreneurial enterprise, the 7-Eleven store, did not result in my parents losing their home. One less obvious reason is that my father's garage is where my first cash-managing safe prototype was born. He and I worked nights and weekends for six months developing, building, and testing a safe that could help speed up the cash-counting process in my stores and the stores of my Money Maker Systems customers. We named the safe Cash Manager and patented the design of how it stored the money by shift and denomination as the cashier dropped the money. Cash Manager safes reduced the time for a manager to count the daily deposit from one hour to ten to fifteen minutes. In 1989, I sold the rights to Cash Manager to Tidel Systems of Carrollton, Texas, and moved to Dallas to join their team.

Dan Petus, a Boeing engineer in Seattle, founded Tidel. A friend of his owned a convenience store that had experienced a number of robberies, so he invented a safe that could only be opened after a time delay had elapsed. It was the first safe capable of dispensing tubes of money, which could only be done every two minutes. These time delays were effective in reducing robberies as the bad guys did not like having to wait through a ten-minute delay to get the door open. After building one in his garage and testing the concept in his friend's store, he made an appointment with 7-Eleven and arranged to have his safe picked up and shipped to Dallas for the meeting. Much to Dan's dismay, he couldn't get the safe working before the freight company picked up the safe. Cash-dispensing safes were obviously meant to be because, in transit to Dallas, his prototype started working again.

In his meeting with 7-Eleven executives, Dan was told that his safe was the stupidest idea ever. He asked for the opportunity to put it in a store for the weekend to confirm how stupid it was. The 7-Eleven manager who received the first safe refused to give it back, and 7-Eleven decided that maybe it was worth taking a closer look. Once convinced that the idea wasn't so stupid after all, 7-Eleven asked for the lead time on seven thousand of them and was quoted six years. (After all, one man building seven thousand safes in his garage should be able to get it done in six years.) They decided they liked the concept enough to offer to buy his company. At the end of Dan's visit to Dallas, when they were finalizing the terms of the sale of his company to 7-Eleven, he asked to include an advance of a couple hundred dollars in the deal. He confessed that he'd only had enough money for the one-way ticket to Dallas.

7-Eleven owned Tidel and supplied over seven thousand timed-access cash controllers, or TACC safes, to their stores. By the time I went to work for Tidel in 1989, they had sold over $100 million worth of TACC units. The TACC unit's primary value was robbery prevention. Although the Cash Manager concept I sold Tidel seemed like a logical product extension to their product line, it never found its way to market. Nevertheless, my life in the safe industry had begun.

Autobank 2000

I left Tidel and went to work for Allied Gary International, a family-owned business that had been around since the 1940s. During my time at Tidel, one of the few individuals who had seen a Cash Manager presentation was Ron Benhart, the loss prevention manger for Amoco Oil. Amoco was buying Autobanks from Allied Gary. The Autobank was a cash-dispensing safe that competed with Tidel's TACC. In 1993, Ron Benhart called and asked if I would come to Chicago to meet with a team that was being assembled at Amoco to reduce the labor of handling cash in their stores. Amoco was developing a concept called cluster management where one store manger would be responsible for three to four stations. In order to execute on the concept, the manager would not have time to count the daily deposits. During the meeting, it was decided that Amoco was hoping for a safe that would count the money as it was deposited. This was a radical new idea in the early 1990s. No product on the market had ever done this before.

As the Allied Gary team set out to invent a new safe for Amoco, we learned a lot about bill validators. The validators that were being used in vending machines and change makers may see twenty-five to one hundred bills per day. In order to use the validator in a safe, it needed to stand up to seven hundred to one thousand bills per day. After a couple missteps with lesser-known bill validator companies, we settled on Mars Electronics, then a division of the Mars candy company that makes Snickers, Mars, and M&Ms. Allied Gary sold six hundred of the first cash-counting safes on the market to Amoco Oil. Mars Electronics embraced the idea of serving this new market. Due to the unmatched quality and reliability of its bill validators and related products, they have since become the de facto standard for the cash-counting safe industry that has developed over the last seventeen years. A large number of retail heavyweights have embraced the concept, and virtually every large armored car company in the world now has a program that includes cash-counting safes.

There are many benefits of cash-counting safes. The first among them for many retailers is the significant labor savings resulting from automating the dangerous and time-consuming process of counting cash deposits in the store. When used in conjunction with an armored car service, nobody at the store level touches cash after it has been deposited into a cash-counting safe. A store manager must enter a PIN, and the armored carrier must present a secure key before the deposit can be collected. No further counting by store personnel is ever required. The increased accountability of having the safe audit every cash transactions makes it very difficult for a dishonest manager to roll deposits at the store level, a scam whereby a store manager steals significant cash from the store, makes a deposit of today's sales receipts, and claims them as yesterday's money.

After the Autobank's success in the marketplace and the success of Brinks' rivaling CompuSafe program, Tidel decided it needed to enter the cash-counting safe market. I was hired as the product manager responsible for developing Tidel's TACC IV and managing the rest of their cash-controller products. At the time, Tidel was much more committed to their ATM division than to their safe division, so, after a few years, I left Tidel for a position with Armor Safe, an up-and-coming company that was laser-focused on one thing, safes that count and dispense money.

Improved Morale and Reduced Employee Theft

Cash fraud can occur when temptation exceeds the risk of getting caught. Employee morale can be damaged in business environments that have loose cash control procedures. In large national companies that operate many locations, keeping track of cash is difficult and expensive. It is common for the store management or cash room management to be responsible for verifying cash sales and deposits by each cashier. A significant challenge of tracking cash shortages is knowing if the cashier, manager, or cash room manager has taken any missing money. Honest cashiers working for dishonest managers no longer have to take the blame for missing deposits they know they deposited. Tight cash control improves morale in cash businesses.

Cash in Transit (Armored Car Service)

The next step in the cash payment system is getting the cash to the bank. The typical approach for cash follows the process described below:

1. The merchant or retailer prepares the cash deposit and places the deposit into a tamper-evident bag.
2. The armored car company arrives at the location and picks up the deposit. The deposit is manifested or signed for by courier. The deposit is signed for an amount "said to contain." This is the amount that the retailer claims is in the deposit. The "said to contain" amount is also the value that is insured during the transit to the cash vault.
3. Once the deposit makes it to the cash processing vault, the deposit is opened under camera and verified. Any difference is communicated back to the merchant.

This system introduces the opportunity for a dispute between the merchant and the verifying vault. I have seen national accounts cancel armored car contracts over disputes between the "said to contain" amount and the amount verified at the vault. During the investigation of a $6,000 discrepancy, the cash-in-transit company admitted that their driver guard probably opened the tamper-evident bag and stole the money. Because the bank processing the deposit did not notify the armored car company that the bag was tampered with, the armored car company attempted to deny the claim. To quote the loss prevention manager of the national account, "This $6,000 claim will cost the armored car company millions in lost revenue from losing our business."

While intelligent safes have increased individual accountability for cash on premise, the above example demonstrates that there is still considerable room for finger-pointing and blame games after the cash leaves the store, which may affect a retailer's deposit total.

The End-to-End Solution: CacheSYSTEM and CacheCONTROL

We have looked at places where fraud can occur throughout the cash payment system. At every handoff, there is an opportunity for fraud. The best approach is to have individual accountability for the cash at every stage and visibility of the cash as it flows from the teenager buying a soda in a convenience store and goes all the way to the merchant's account. This is exactly what Armor Safe Technologies' CacheSYSTEM and CacheCONTROL secure-hosted software provides.

CacheCONTROL began as an application written on top of Armor's existing Bi-Comm spec, a protocol that allows other devices to communicate with Armor's safes. Developed initially for the South African market by Protea Coin, South Africa's largest armored car service provider, CacheCONTROL has been widely available in that market for four years. It has undergone numerous improvements over the years, adding sophisticated use of radio-frequency identification (RFID) tagged cassettes, software to automated cassette processing in an armored car carrier's vault, and an application for setting up funding from Armor safes to merchant's bank accounts. Today, CacheCONTROL is available in the United States as well, and other markets are on the horizon. The following describes the cash payment path with CacheCONTROL:

- The merchant's cash is collected at the point of sale by its cashiers.
- The cashiers make deposits into a CacheSYSTEM or CacheNET safe. The local site is given immediate feedback in the form of a receipt of the deposit. A secure IP packet containing transaction details is immediately sent to the hosted CacheCONTROL server.
- In the retailer's store, the site manager can run a number of simple intuitive reports, including user, shift, and end-of-day reports in order to assist in managing the business at the store level.
- Meanwhile, the CacheCONTROL server compiles all of the deposits for this location as well as all the merchant's other locations.
- CacheCONTROL makes it possible for the merchant to receive credit from the safe daily, even while the cash deposit still resides in its Armor safe.
- The armored car company picks up the cash from the location in secure, RFID cassettes to be transported to the cash vault.
- The cassettes arrive at the cash vault. The RFID tag is read, describing the location from which the cassette originated and other details. The CacheCONTROL server knows the value to expect in the cassette because it has been updated constantly as the deposits are made.
- The vault cashiers process the deposit blind (without knowing what

the safe expected the deposit to be) to ensure the cassette made it to the vault and keys the amounts for the cassette into the CacheCONTROL application.

- CacheCONTROL compiles all of the deposits and prepares the bank report for granting credit to the merchant's account.

The advantage and beauty of this system is that, at every step along the payment path, the cash is visible. In essence, cash has been digitized. The merchant, armored car company, and bank have real-time visibility of the cash in the payment system. When cash goes missing, the end-to-end solution clearly exposes the point at which it does so.

This is really just the beginning of the future of cash management and another radical change in our industry's dynamics. It is how progressive retailers are handling cash today and how most retailers will handle cash in the years ahead. We are, in many ways, "changing the way the world counts cash."

CHAPTER FOUR

FIGHTING THE UNDERTOW OF CHECK FRAUD

JOE GREGORY, ORBOGRAPH, AND BOB JONES, THE SANTA FE GROUP

SWIMMERS and surfers love the beach for many reasons. Surfers crave the challenge and danger of the waves while beachgoers simply enjoy the warmth of the sun and enter the ocean water for an occasional cool down. For all, one warning is common, "Watch out for the undertow!" To stay in the spirit of tsunamis and surfing, we'd like to start with an analogy that check fraud is like the undertow of the ocean. From a distance, everything at the beach looks under control, calm and safe. Even when the undertow is strong, a safe beachgoer can enter a few feet into the ocean and simply enjoy the rush of water around his feet. One could argue this point in check processing as well. Many banks have made their check imaging platform decisions. Check volumes are declining, and many banks have systems in place for check fraud prevention. What else needs to be done? Aren't we safe from the undertow of check fraud?

The experienced swimmer or surfer knows the danger of the ocean while the unsuspecting casual beachgoer can be caught off guard. One minute, you're splashing happily in the surf. The next, you're being dragged out to sea at top speed.

Check fraud losses can happen just as fast. Minimal fraudulent activity may be experienced for months, but then, one day, a fraud ring or a large check hits. Wham! Six-figure losses!

A Problem That Just Won't Go Away

The ABA's Deposit Account Fraud Survey is the financial industry's most trusted report on check fraud losses, providing current statistics classified by bank asset size. The most recent version was published in November 2009 and is based on one hundred and seventy survey responses from financial institutions in the United States. These institutions report on actual losses incurred during the 2008 calendar year.

The primary headline in this report is that estimated check fraud losses topped $1 billion, the first time since the ABA began collecting data in 1998 (1997 data). Total estimated fraud losses were up by 5 percent, totaling $1.024 billion, compared to an estimated $969 million in 2006. Banks were able to prevent approximately 90 percent of the fraud exposure ($11.4 billion), but were working harder to do so, as the number of fraud cases increased by 35 percent (761,000 from 561,000). As in the two previous surveys, returned deposited items (35 percent), counterfeit checks (30 percent), and forgeries (22 percent) made up most of the losses.

The responses from community banks (assets greater than $500 million), midsized banks ($500 million to $4.9 billion), regional banks ($5 billion to $49.9 billion), and super regional/money center banks (greater than $50 billion) offered several surprises and set expectations for the upcoming years:

- Community banks reported 41 percent of their losses were from counterfeit checks, far higher than the other categories, whose losses were in the 20 to 30 percent range.
- Community bank forgery losses were 13 percent lower than midsized and regional banks (17 percent and 20 percent, respectively) and marginally higher than super regional/money center banks (12 percent).
- Seventy-four percent of the fraud losses dealt with personal accounts. This number is expected to drop as personal check volumes decline faster than business check writing.
- As float disappears due to expedited check clearing, so too is the expected demise of kiting. In 2008, kiting was estimated at only 6 percent of all losses. Unfortunately, kiting will still exist to some degree due to corporate sweep accounts and weekend float.

Orbograph also completed its own fraud assessment survey in 2009. Orbograph's survey was completed via e-mail with seventy-five respondents. The results were slightly more conservative than ABA's, perhaps due to their reluctance of full disclosure to an outside vendor. See loss comparisons below:

Asset Size	<500M	500M-4B	4B-50B	50B+
Total Orbograph Respondents providing losses	12 of 18	19 of 26	12 of 18	8 of 13
ABA Respondents[1]	49	81	24	16
Orbograph Mean	$60,950	$69,579	$752,928	
ABA Mean[1]	$15,219	**$106,716**	**$741,224**	**$30,708,003**
Orbograph Median	$15,000	$21,000	$211,000	
ABA Median[1]	$12,554	**$47,011**	**$684,460**	**$8,324,297**

[1]ABA number of respondents, ABA mean, and ABA median obtained from 2009 ABA Deposit Account Fraud Survey Report

Confirming the ongoing fraud problem, the Association for Financial Professionals (AFP) published a report in March 2009 highlighting 71 percent of the corporations interviewed experienced attempted or actual payments fraud. Of these, 91 percent were victims of check fraud. This report also highlighted problems dealing with altered payees and altered employee paychecks in addition to counterfeits. Not surprisingly, larger corporations were more prone to exposure than smaller companies were, as 80 percent of $1 billion-plus companies were victims to payment fraud versus only 63 percent under $1 billion.

Some analysts think losses are actually higher and not because banks withhold them. Rather, banks don't always categorize losses the same way. For example, overdraft losses may well include unreported fraud. Though a bank may choose not to participate in the biennial ABA surveys, it should consider using the ABA's loss definitions so it will be able to benchmark its experience with the banks that do report. Additionally, as the number of checks converted to ACH transactions continues to grow, losses in cross-channel fraud are many times now reported under "other or ACH."

It is interesting to note that neither the AFP survey nor the bank surveys estimate a total impact of check fraud. Certain sources cite the overall impact is potentially ten times that of the $1 billion presented, as merchant losses on goods stolen by fraudsters is essentially absorbed as a cost of doing business. If you bring in losses from credit cards at an industry level that approaches $22 billion, it's hard to see how certain businesses can make a profit these days!

Cost of Doing Business Mentality

Industry activity to address the check fraud crisis seems to be accelerating. Although many community banks claim minimal or no losses, many have implemented at least limited systems to maintain proactive customer perception on fraud prevention.

Large financial institutions typically have several complex systems in place that are often implemented in silos. They continue to chip away at trimming losses. Ultimately, you have to ask, "Is check fraud the redheaded stepchild?" Many bankers have simply taken a cost of doing business approach to check fraud. Minimizing risk in other payments channels and online banking fraud might be considered greater compliance and PR exposure. For example, if an online banking system is hacked and account data is penetrated, the negative publicity is significantly greater then if a $2,000 customer check is counterfeited. Simply refund the account, and it is resolved!

Many banks see fraud problems as being unique to their situation. The illusion of check fraud is that, although you feel you are on a different island than others, nearly every bank in your asset size is on the same ocean. The check fraud undertow is only a few feet away from "knocking you on your keister."

The Clearing Rules with Image Exchange

The changes to funds availability as Part 229, Availability of Funds and Collection of Checks (Regulation CC), will add a new dynamic to the fraud mix for 2010 and beyond. These changes essentially make all checks local, a good thing from the standpoint of customers and float. But it also gives a fraudster the ability to withdraw funds the next day on fraudulent items!

Fraudsters may be able to exploit certain environments because there is still a one- to two-day delay in returns processing of fraudulent items. New technologies and refined workflows will need to be implemented in order to close this gap.

An interesting check clearing rule that has been around for some time to address the reality of remotely created checks (RCC) is Rule 8, which essentially transfers liability for a third-party initiated check (RCC) or preauthorized draft (PAD) from the paying bank to the depository bank. The rule was originally designed to deal with demand drafts issued by fraudulent merchants.

One could argue that these new rules provide better protection to the paying bank, providing incentives for investment into stronger on-us check protection. Paying banks can now potentially exploit these rules and push more losses to the bank of first deposit (BOFD). This illustrates the need for greater cooperation and collaboration as a necessity for banks to support one another.

When the BITS Fraud Reduction Steering Committee was organized in 1998, the members quickly reached consensus that fraud is not a competitive issue. They agreed to freely share what they were losing, where they were losing it, and how they were losing it. They recognized that data exchange inevitably leads to the identification of best practices. They also agreed that fraud is a zero-sum game. If Bank A installs a tool or develops a business practice that detects fraud attempts, its neighbor, Credit Union B will find its losses increasing if it doesn't adopt a similar strategy.

Technology Evolution

A number of technologies have advanced significantly over the past two years that can help this greater cause in fraud prevention. These include analytic engines, image analysis, and deposit fraud integration. Each component on its own has strengths and weaknesses.

- New analytic engines can now better filter suspects to a more manageable level, but fraud investigators still require the check image for the final decision.
- Improved image analysis brings amazing accuracy to automated signature authentication and counterfeit detection. Additionally, certain vendors can successfully process IRDs , RCCs, and PADs seamlessly. Unfortunately, image-only approaches cannot detect all forms of fraud.
- Deposit fraud systems can now integrate a wide range of customer data and transaction activity for online, real-time account verification; flagging; and behavior analysis. Additionally, these systems can be used across the payment spectrum for debit card, ATM, online banking transactions, and account openings. The drawback to this approach is

that it is dependent on historical data and account updates provided from banks subscribing to the system.

Leveraging the Clearing Infrastructure in Fraud Prevention

The old saying goes, "Something is better than nothing." This adage certainly applies to check fraud prevention. But is there really an approach that can dramatically reduce losses and risk throughout the financial services industry? We believe same-day, interbank fraud detection and notification is such an approach. This strategy simply starts with a cooperative model between financial institutions that have significant volumes of checks being exchanged.

Same-day, interbank fraud prevention works by placing an integrated analytics engine with image analysis at the paying bank for immediate processing of incoming items. Orbograph's approach incorporates a real-time fraud solution called Sereno, which incorporates Multi-Source Correlation Modeling. This approach works in real time on incoming items from multiple inclearing sources. The key to a successful approach is low-suspect rate/high-detection rate. The blending of analytics and image analysis drives false positive rates near 0.2 to 0.5 percent and can be less with dollar thresholding.

This combination would enable the paying bank to send immediate notifications through its clearing provider or returns channel so the BOFD can place holds on funds with doubtful collectability. The end result is a fraudster that will be unable to withdraw funds the following morning!

The feasibility of this model is dependent on cooperation. Banks and their trading partners need to implement a similar approach in order to see a mutually beneficial process. Remember that your on-us fraud is their deposit fraud. The impact of which can be significant if done prior to posting at the paying bank. As a side benefit, this infrastructure can also used simultaneously for over-the-counter on-us items to halt outgoing cash on fraudulent cashed checks.

Conclusion

For the first time in memory, Check21 and image exchange has represented law overtaking technology. Although image presentment has made paper-based security features obsolete, new clearing rules with image exchange offer unprecedented opportunities to detect fraud earlier in the payment cycle. With this early identification, if shared with its counterparty, the depositing bank will never completely eliminate check fraud, but will make the banking system a much safer and calmer place to live.

CHAPTER FIVE

THE FRAUD TSUNAMI: BEST ACTICES FOR FIGHTING THE STORM AND ACHIEVING MAXIMUM SECURITY ONLINE.

ORI EISEN, 41ST PARAMETER

Executive Summary

A layered approach to online security helps balance a user's desire to transact conveniently against enterprise needs to reduce the risk of fraudulent activity. However, no single technology can effectively meet the nuanced needs of both users and online enterprises. While regulations have focused on "user authentication," recent FFIEC guidance and real-world applications call for a layered approach to security that deploys overt, real-time methods, agent-less device identification (CDI), forensic analysis, and data masking.

Both real-time and time-delayed fraud detection systems have a role in combating internet fraud, but how can they be used in concert with one another for even greater lift in detection and prevention? This chapter discusses how organizations should best employ real-time and time-delayed systems, in addition to human intelligence, to achieve maximum security online.

The critically important process of account registration or enrollment processes are particularly vulnerable. Because true identities of the users simply cannot be discerned online with total certainty, this chapter addresses a realistic blueprint for a security schema that brings together an array of risk management methodologies, best practices, and technology. This schema helps produce a security environment that offers a convenient user experience, while providing accurate risk assessment during the login, throughout the session, and prior to the execution of transactions.

Many businesses that operate today on demand and in real-time are limiting their ability to detect, prevent, and recover their fraud losses. This chapter may trigger a change in the very business model of such enterprises, helping to maximize profits, protect the customer experience with convenience and privacy, and extend the life-time-value of every user, while minimizing fraud and operational losses as well as customer inconvenience and attrition.

The Threat Environment

Knowing that all it takes is the right credential presentment to gain access to lucrative online accounts, fraudsters have been devising methods to obtain this information. In effect, they are practicing the age-old art of impersonation in new, electronic forms using techniques such as:

Phishing – Sending fraudulent e-mails that appear to be from the user's financial institution or a merchant to lure victims to provide their credentials.

Pharming – Poisoning the DNS cache on the user's device so it appears to access the correct URL, when in reality it is redirecting the browser to a spoofed site; this can also be done to a DNS server, which poisons an entire region.

Spoofed Site – Presenting a link to a fake site that looks and feels like the original site.

Malware – Installing malicious software on the user's device to collect information through keyboard logging, screenshots and file searches.

Man-In-The-Middle (MITM) – Passing a user's device through a proxy that is privy to all traffic between the user and the Web site, including the user's credentials.

Session Hijacking – Using an authenticated session (after the user authenticated) to mimic a new session and conduct transactions from the compromised account.

IVR Spoofing – Faking Interactive Voice Response (IVR) systems that call on users to dial and provide account information and/or credentials.

Cookie Theft – Theft of software cookies used to assume the victim's digital identity.

This list is far from complete, yet the point remains: given the human ingenuity of the fraudsters, they will always find a way to glean information from unsuspecting users. Therefore, it is imperative that compromised credentials do not turn into compromised accounts.

We're Fighting Humans, Not Machines

Before the security issue can be solved, it is critical to understand the kind of issues the online industry faces. One cannot assume that the problem can be solved through technology alone.

Take for instance, the anti-virus world where hackers write malicious code used to infect the host. By design, anti-virus detection software is blind to new attacks and is invariably one attack behind the latest scheme. After a new virus is detected, usually by humans, it is inspected down to its "DNA," and a detection algorithm is devised to alert when this exact code is executed again. At this point, every replica of the same virus will exhibit the same code execution, thereby allowing a digital guard to search for it and quarantine it upon engagement.

Why then can't the same digital guard find the next virus, inspect its "DNA" and write the inoculation code? The reason is very simple—the fight is against humans, not machines. While some heuristics allow antivirus mutations to be detected even if the exact code was not executed, the true problem lies with new attacks that have never been seen before.

The main challenge in defending against online fraud attacks is the ingenuity of the humans behind them and the fact that enterprises most often try to counter them solely with machine intelligence.

False Positives and False Negatives—A Necessary Evil

In the end, a site must be built to conduct business. Otherwise, it will be incredibly secure, yet provide little or no profit. Any security measure deployed to millions must be easy and convenient to use, which in most cases, also makes it easy to foil. For that reason alone, there must be some measures of balance between convenience, security, and privacy, in the form of false positives and false negatives.

> **False Positive**: A good user transaction declined under the suspicion of being fraudulent

> **False Negative**: A fraudulent user transaction approved while not sounding the alarm

Both occurrences end up hurting the company as well as the customer.

THE MARKET ENVIRONMENT

Security Based on the User is Only as Secure as the User

Regardless of how often customers are educated about online security, they will always be susceptible to attacks. Therefore, a security solution based on users inherently casts users as the weakest link.

Conditioning the Users

One widely-employed attempt to reinforce the weakest link is to train users to expect certain visual measures when they act in a certain way. While this provides a positive reassurance to valid users, it tells the fraudster when they have tripped the alarm, hence, helping them to reverse engineer the system.

Likewise, conditioning users to expect challenge questions is another matter. Should the online site consider taking away those challenge questions one day, it will create a new set of issues.

For instance, consider a watermark that users view as the site's seal of authenticity. Once users associate this seal with their security, there could be a time when a browser will not load the seal due to technical reasons and will show an error placeholder in its place.

Now, consider an attack that will show this red "X" instead of trying to mimic the site's seal. Most users will think there is a browser technical issue rather than suspect fraud.

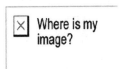

Internet communication is a two-way street, and just as the sites do not know who is presenting the credentials, the users do not know whether they landed on the authentic Web page.

As the lifeblood of online business, a positive customer experience is critical to a holistic security strategy. Changing the behavior of millions of customers is no small feat, given the time and expense needed to educate them—both of which are often vastly underestimated.

Changing user behavior even once is difficult; changing it time and again to stay ahead of new fraud schemes becomes nearly impossible.

Balancing Convenience, Security, and Privacy

It is important to recognize that giving users "some" credentials—a way of identifying themselves online—increases their sense of security and trust with a Web site.

Credentials need to be user-friendly, as opposed to providing an account ID and password that are both secure, yet difficult to remember, and therefore are only artificially secure. After all, users are not machines.

To illustrate, study the following account ID and password for two minutes, then look away and try to recall them both.

Account ID = a3GH67db889Ikl
Password = 6yGtrf44sedw67

As you can see, this is nearly impossible. While a long and case-sensitive password may achieve security, the inability to remember it will cause great frustration and inconvenience. Furthermore, complex passwords will ultimately result in locked-out users and thousands of expensive call center requests to reset passwords. Some enterprises allow password reset online, which then opens another door for the fraudster. How does the enterprise know who initiated this password reset?

Humans are wired a certain way and are pre-disposed to remember shorter and more meaningful passwords. Hence, sites should allow users to select passwords they can relate to and memorize. However, additional layers of security are needed to achieve the necessary balance.

Effective security must be both easy and secure.

THE ONLINE SECURITY ENVIRONMENT

Security Options: Authentication is Not a Silver Bullet

A common misconception is that stronger authentication solves the security issue. In light of the growing sophistication and complexity of fraud schemes, we know this to be far from true. Just as the police employ both overt and covert agents, so should any security system. Examples of how overt and covert methods complement each other in life include:

- Police: Street Officer and Undercover Detective
- Casino: Pit Boss and Backroom Operations
- Airport: TSA Agents and Air Marshalls

Together, a synergy is created that offers two safety nets of protection from any catastrophic failure by each individual component.

KBA: A Catch 22?

To foster the additional authentication of suspicious transactions, many organizations use Knowledge Based Authentication (KBA). With KBA, the user is prompted to answer additional questions that only he/she should be able to answer.

However, such assumptions can be dangerous. Should the fraudster answer the additional KBA, often no other lines of defense exist before the transaction is completed, resulting in a false sense of security.

It is critical to determine when to invoke the questions in order to retain any value. If challenge questions are posed only when risky transactions are requested, one must ask, "Why weren't the questions posed ahead of time to prevent an unauthorized user from even getting into the account?"

On the other hand, if the KBA is part of the initial login process and the user cannot answer correctly, he/she will be denied access. If the question is answered correctly, the user is granted full access to the account. Either way, the risks are the same.

Online Security Best Practices: Authentication and Beyond

Thus far, we have addressed the following:

- True online authentication is not feasible, as the internet is not designed for it.
- The ultimate fight is against humans, not machines.
- Users should play a role in your security strategy, yet should not solely be relied upon.
- Users are not secure by design.

Given these conditions, the following strategies for enterprise security should be considered:

1. Real-Time Security at the Front-End – Provides ironclad doors at the front-end based on strong authentication.
2. Time-Delayed Security on the Back-End – Provides ironclad doors at the back–end that do not let any transaction execute until exhaustive analysis is performed.
3. Combination of Real-Time and Time-Delayed Security – Decisions are based on what is possible and best to perform at each juncture of the transaction's lifecycle. This involves human intelligence in addition to sensitive data masking.

There are a number of schemes that would not be detected with only real-time systems, namely:

- Detecting one device logging into multiple accounts
- Detecting device manipulations, cookie theft, or session hijacking

- Detecting offline fraud that results from fraudulent account access (wires or counterfeit checks)

It is impossible to detect the link between these events and fraudulent online access, because they occur out of sequence and in different channels with long delays between the occurrences.

The Security Trinity: Three Critical Questions

At the core, three primary questions must be addressed when a user attempts to login, view and potentially transact online:

1. Should the site allow the user to login to the account? (Authentication)
2. Should the site monitor whether one device is accessing multiple user accounts even without transacting? (Account Surveillance)
3. Should the site allow the transaction(s) to execute and money to leave the account? (Transaction Risk Monitoring)

The first question lends itself to a real-time check, in which the user is either authenticated or not.

The second question relates to transaction authorization and is not required to be answered in real-time or during the session. Rather, it can and should be determined post-session. This question should be answered with "shades of gray," and if necessary, prompt human intervention for final verification.

The third question reveals whether a perpetrator is lurking and waiting to see when accounts have high balances, or alternatively, whether they are gleaning sensitive customer information from online document images to commit offline fraud such as check counterfeit or siphoning accounts via ACH. For that reason it is critical to mask sensitive customer and account data in addition to quickly detecting and containing such attacks.

Negative Lists

No matter how rich the negative list is, when a fraudulent user receives the error message, they know they did something they should not have. There is a diminishing marginal utility to a negative list, as the fraudster was just told what not to do. Remember we are fighting humans and not machines, so the perpetrators are likely to try again with a different set of credentials that are not (yet) on the negative list.

Naturally, after a fraud case is confirmed, the fraud investigators can and should update the front door negative list to try and prevent these credentials from coming in again. This effort is both Sisyphean in nature and reactive.

Of course, this is not to imply a company should not attempt to stop known fraudsters at the door. Rather, anticipating future moves by invisibly monitoring behavior is equally important. In every successful fraud attack, the perpetrator slipped through the front gates and any back-end fraud detection processes that were in place. Adding layered security to the transaction lifecycle provides more interception points.

Masking Visible Sensitive Customer Information

To determine the usability and security of a site, a detailed security audit must be performed. It should include all sensitive customer information and scanned documents that contain potential points of vulnerability, such as online checks, statements, and previous transactions details. Account information should be truncated. For example, if the full account number is 123456789, the visible information shown would be xxxxx6789.

Likewise, other customer data such as address, signature and potentially driver's license or SSN, are also shown on online check images. Given the anonymity of the internet, all sensitive customer information should be completely or partially masked. Most legitimate users do not need to view their own sensitive information. Yet, by leaving the information viewable, it provides everything a perpetrator needs to counterfeit a check or siphon the account.

Let Humans Do What They Do Best and Machines Do What They Do Best

We have established that real-time systems cannot and should not detect all possible fraudulent scenarios, thus, separation of duties must be determined. It is not feasible for the front-end to conduct back-end investigations.

The back-end, inherently, has additional time and human intelligence. Therefore, it should feed the negative lists that serve as the first line of defense. This approach also helps when a wrong value is placed in a negative list, which can wreak havoc in real time, such as blocking an IP address from a popular

Internet Service Provider. While an attack coming from a popular IP address may be mathematically "right" to place in the negative list, the overall implications would be disastrous.

The Medium Is the Message

Part of setting up any security perimeter includes limiting multiple login attempts originating from the same source. If the wrong password is provided three times on an account, the account should be frozen until direct support from the company is obtained. Alternatively, multiple successful logins originating from the same source into different accounts are equally suspect and must be monitored as well.

The velocity needs to be monitored on multiple vectors, such as IP address, login ID, and device ID. All of which require database seek time and CPU processing cycles that can consequently delay the customer experience.

When one point of origin is linked to many accounts, the medium is the message. When one source is attempting, or has actually gained access to multiple accounts, there is good reason to suspect it as fraud.

Proposed Best Practices

Best practice employs user name and password authentication, and adds a check into a negative list based on intrinsic values (such as device ID, account ID, or high-risk countries). The error message in case of a "hit" should be as "vanilla-flavored" as possible, so as to not tell the potential crook why they are being denied. For example: *Our Web site is currently experiencing heavy traffic. Please try again later.* It is then recommended that the business contact the account holder to validate this activity for customer service reasons and proactive fraud detection.

A holistic strategy combining real-time with time-delayed security methods results in maximum security online with minimal inconvenience to users and minimal exposure of an institution's security strategy to the fraudsters. The best practices should focus on the following core activities:

- Overt authentication on the front-end,
- Agent-less client device identification (CDI) and surveillance that

allows for monitoring of fraudsters presenting credentials as well as their site navigation,

- Covert transaction risk monitoring, and
- Overt data masking to obscure/hide sensitive customer information.

Final Thoughts

A holistic security framework consists of three areas of risk focus: authentication at login, transaction monitoring, and account and session surveillance. Each area is chartered with one mission and does not rely on the others. By applying these three together, you achieve a sum that is greater than the value of each area on its own. In effect, you have emulated an environment that relies on complex assessment of both initial recognition and subsequent behavior to determine whether authenticated activity should be intercepted.

The internet was not designed for true user authentication. Given that the ultimate fight is against humans, not machines, we must prepare for an ongoing war against internet fraud and identity theft. Combining real-time and time-delayed security with intervention from company investigators allows an organization to let users take part in the security ecosystem, without hinging the strategy upon them. Real-time plus time-delayed security delivers maximum security online.

Chapter Six

Universal Biometric Identity Verification To Curtail Fraud

Michael Milgramm, IdentaZone Inc.

FRAUD, fraud, fraud …These days we are bombarded with messages of financial and computer fraud everywhere we look. As computers, networks, and other automated systems permeate every part of our everyday lives, fraud rapidly becomes a common household term. The definition of what constitutes such fraud, however, becomes ever more complex with the ingenuity of people who intend to deceive, misrepresent, destroy, steal information, or cause harm to others by accessing information through deceptive and illegal means.

Types of fraud vary and can be very complex or quite simple. Here are examples of fraudulent schemes:

- Advance-Fee Fraud Schemes;
- Business/Employment Schemes;
- Counterfeit Check Schemes;
- Credit/Debit Card Fraud;
- Freight Forwarding/Reshipping;
- Investment Fraud;
- Non-delivery of Goods/Service
- Online Auction/Retail;
- Phony Escrow Services;
- Ponzi/Pyramid Schemes
- Spoofing/Phishing;

- Identity Theft.

Lets examine one of the currently known schemes.

Identity Theft

Identity theft occurs when someone appropriates another's personal information without their knowledge to commit theft or fraud. Identity theft is a vehicle for perpetrating other types of fraud schemes. Typically, the victim is led to believe he/she is divulging sensitive personal information to a legitimate business, sometimes as a response to an e-mail solicitation to update billing or membership information, or as an application to a fraudulent internet job posting.

Identity theft can happen to anyone, and the revealed information may be used in multiple ways. For example, victim's credit card digits could be stolen and used to make online purchases; a thief could impersonate the victim to obtain a loan in the victim's name; a felon could commit a crime and pretend to be the victim when caught; or someone could use the victim's personal information to apply for a job. Credit/debit card numbers can also be stolen from unsecured Web sites. Based on Federal Trade Commission complaint data, credit card fraud constitutes 26 percent of all reported cases, loan fraud constitutes 5 percent, and bank fraud accounts for another 17 percent. Other types of cases include, utilities fraud (18%), employment fraud (12%), government fraud (9%) and others (13%).

Even a brief look at the statistical data allows us to grasp the enormous extent of this calamity.

- There were **10 million victims** of identity theft in 2008 in the United States (Javelin Strategy and Research, 2009).
- **One in every ten** U.S. consumers has already been victimized by identity theft (Javelin Strategy and Research, 2009).
- **Seven percent** of identity theft victims had their information stolen to commit **medical identity theft**.
- **Approximately 25.9 million Americans** carry insurance obtained as a result of identity theft (as of September 2008, from Javelin Strategy and Research, 2009).

- In 2008, existing account fraud in the U.S. totaled **$31 billion** (Javelin Strategy and Research, 2009).
- Businesses across the world lose **$221 billion** a year because of identity theft (Aberdeen Group).
- The mean cost per victim is **$500** (Javelin Strategy and Research, 2009).

The above-described enormous financial losses suffered as a result of identity theft, constitute only a portion of overall losses from constantly growing and evolving problems of financial fraud. Moreover, financial fraud is rapidly becoming the new turf of international and organized crime.

To combat the mounting threat of financial fraud, an increasing number of joint cyber-crime task forces have been established across the country. Over the past year, more than fifty such task forces have either been established or significantly augmented with resources from numerous federal, state, and local agencies. Federal Bureau of Investigation has built a whole new set of technological and investigative capabilities and partnerships "to address cyber crime in a coordinated and cohesive manner." Internet Crime Complaint Center (IC3), which is a partnership between the National White Collar Crime Center (NW3C) and the FBI, has been established as a vehicle to receive, develop, and refer criminal complaints regarding the rapidly expanding arena of cyber-crime. Multiple individual businesses have implemented a wide variety of their own techniques to forestall financial fraud. Victims of ID theft must contact multiple agencies to resolve the fraud: 66 percent interact with financial institutions; 40 percent contact credit bureaus; 35 percent seek help from law enforcement; 22 percent deal with debt collectors; 20 percent work with identity theft assistance services; and 13 percent contact the Federal Trade Commission (Javelin Strategy and Research, 2009). However, despite this continuous and often coordinated effort, dollar loss from financial fraud has more than doubled between 2008 and 2009 from $265 million to $559.70 million.

The more advanced information systems become, the more advanced are the criminals who try to penetrate them. Fraud can now be committed through various media, including <u>mail</u>, <u>wire</u>, <u>phone</u>, the <u>internet</u>, and so forth. Neither passwords nor encryption can guarantee positive identification. Accurate identification and authentication, especially in combination with encryption and other technologies, is the only way to curtail fraud. In other words, we believe that it is impossible to prevail in this fight against fraud without utilizing biometric technology.

Let us briefly consider the field of biometrics. Biometrics is an automated method of recognizing a person based on a physiological or behavioral characteristic. Biometric technologies are rapidly becoming the foundation of an extensive array of highly secure identification and personal verification solutions. Several considerations present themselves when one considers using biometric technologies for identification:

- *Universality*: To be usable, a particular biometric characteristic has to be present in every person. Therefore, it should be considered that some people do not have scan-able fingerprints and, thus, are not suitable for biometric solutions based on fingerprint technology.
- *Uniqueness*: Generally, no two people have identical biometric characteristics. However, identical twins are hard to distinguish.
- *Permanence*: Selected characteristics should not vary with time. One should keep in mind, however, that a person's face, for example, may change with age.
- *Collectability*: Selected characteristics must be easily collectible and measurable.
- *Performance*: The identification method must be selected such that it delivers accurate results under varied environmental circumstances.
- *Acceptability*: Biometric data collection routine must be accepted by the general public. Generally, non-intrusive methods are more acceptable.
- *Circumvention*: The technology should be difficult to deceive.

While many biometric security specialists advocate immediate use of biometric technologies to curtail fraud, such technologies have not yet gained widespread acceptability. Multiple reasons are to blame. First, while biometric applications continue to improve, a small possibility of error remains. Different biometric applications have different thresholds of accuracy, in both obtaining the data and in its processing. Moreover, each application has its own requirement for quality and size of obtained images. Therefore, each application necessitates its own scanning equipment. Accordingly, at present, interoperability does not characterize use of biometric technologies. Moreover, based on the current stage of development of biometric technology only the simultaneous use of multiple biometric technologies can provide for an accurate identification.

To date, however, the field of biometrics remains the land of few standards when it comes to end to end solutions. Part of the reason is the sheer complexity of biometric industry. Consider its taxonomy: the number of layers between a scanner reading off biometric information (called an access layer) and the database granting access to information could range between five and seven. More so, the range of biometric devices and applications is growing in geometric progression. What was fresh and cutting edge today becomes obsolete and cumbersome tomorrow, and many larger institutions in need of secure access—government organizations, financial institutions, and high-tech installations—are caught playing catch up and developing their own biometric systems that are expensive to scale and maintain.

A typical biometric installation today is a proprietary affair where biometric elements have been integrated with internal security systems via an expensive process of proprietary system integration. Biometric elements are connected via software extensions into a proprietary biometric database, which in turn is connected via proprietary software extensions into security databases. In such a setup, the proprietary nature of software code linking biometric and non-biometric security elements doesn't add value to the overall impregnability of the system. It mostly makes adding new security elements and communication between various pieces of the security system difficult to execute and expensive to maintain. More so, the proprietary nature of biometric security systems eliminates the opportunity for two financial institutions to safely share biometric data in the same fashion that today they share financial data.

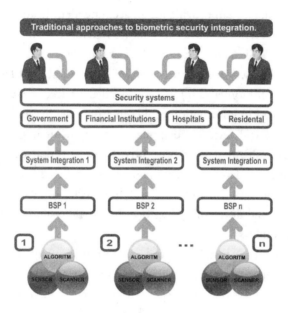

A novel solution currently being offered is a universal biometric identity verification system Independent Security Server® (INdSS) that is based on Independent Biometric Identification System(IBIS) technologies. In general, the novel system consists of two parts:

- Biometric Repository, i.e., the database; and
- Independent Security Server® (INdSS), i.e., the middleware combining the benefits of biometric and security applications.

Biometric Repository

Biometric Repository is a universal repository for biometric profiles. The Biometric Repository holds only encoded biometric templates. While biometric profiles are stored within the repository, each individual user is defined with a PIN. This PIN is assigned based on its unique authentication characteristics. The interaction between consumer profile and biometric information happens based on this PIN.

INdSS Middleware

INdSS Middleware is an "interpreter" that allows for interoperability between various biometric technologies and security systems.

What exactly is middleware, and why is this proposed middleware so flexible to use and integrate? The middleware operates between the security application layer, e.g., an existing security system developed by any third party, and the biometric logic layer. INdSS middleware provides a solid foundation for development of secure biometrics- enabled applications.

The middleware can be easily integrated into any third-party environment, because it does not depend on any type of business and recognizes only two responses: "yes" and "no."

Another unique aspect of INdSS is that its unified identity verification principal is applicable to multiple applications.

The middleware works with all available biometric devices and supports unlimited factor authentication, thus enabling full interoperability of the system.

INdSS supports every existing biometric, security and software standard, communication protocol, and encryptions method, and provides a unified method of principal registration and profile storage. Further, because of its modular construction, the middleware allows the administrator to quickly integrate and optimize new biometric technologies. The system is optimized for high performance, scalability and reliability; the middleware enables a desired security level by supporting the optimal mix of biometric characteristics used for identification.

There are two main processes executed by the middleware: enrollment and identification.

Enrollment is one of the most important aspects of a well-functioning biometric system. Quality of the enrollment process has the most bearing on the quality of the identification process, and consequently, on any control over access to funds, critical information, and so on.

It is the interoperability of the enrollment as well as the identification and authentication processes that makes the INdSS system truly functional, in spite of certain shortcomings of current biometric solutions. One of the key features of this system is its flexibility of allowing for selection of biometric scanners that best fit the needs of the client, individual characteristics of the person being identified, and specific cost concerns. Further, selection of such biometric equipment is done regardless of whether the person to be identified is an employee or a client of the user-company. Thus, within one organization the system can accommodate different departments with different biometric needs. Moreover, different biometric technologies can be used within the same department. This approach is one of the main advantages of the novel system that enables the system to encompass a larger number of potential users. Further, this system is a definitive answer to the critics of biometrics who insist that biometric technologies are not ready for today's market.

If enrollment process is critical in delivering correct biometric information into the system, the identification and authentication process is the backbone of the system that allows for the end user to execute authentication using biometric factors.

Additionally, it is important to mention that INdSS is operable to utilize any combination of biometric factors, e.g., fingerprint and iris recognition or iris and facial recognition, depending on the required level of security.

Following is a typical example of a user-authentication process. An end user trying to access his/her funds in a financial institution would first request access and submit biometric data for authentication. The middleware receives the biometric data, compares it to the PIN stored in the biometric repository, and either grants or denies the access.

This process can be illustrated by the following exemplary steps:

1. I am looking to get access to my bank account.
2. No worries, but let's make sure that you are who you say you are first.
3. Yes, we confirm that you are have an entry in the Biometric database.
4. Your PIN matches.
5. Your bank account access is granted.

To further emphasize the use of this novel solution system in fraud prevention, lets consider another example. Assuming a particular security department or organization has information about a certain person of interest, a PIN is created based on this information and is placed into a security database. The security personnel can further select a particular countermeasure in case the PIN is recognized. Such countermeasures may include a text message alert to a predetermined employee, a system block, a police alert, and so on. When a person tries to access the banking system using the biometric process, his/her biometric data is checked against the security database, and if the PIN is matched, an appropriate countermeasure is taken.

To summarize, the proposed new system provides a multi-layer platform independence.

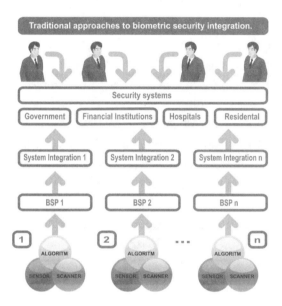

Specifically, the system:

- Supports any market because the system is independent from all specific applications, thus allowing it to ignore differences in solutions while servicing different markets.
- Utilizes any available biometric identity verification system, and, most importantly, enables integration of different brands and types of biometric systems as well as unlimited factor authentication.
- Is completely modular in that it enables the use of virtually any desirable encryption technology that can be as robust as desired for various applications.
- Allows developers of biometric technologies, security systems, and databases to continue upgrading their solutions, all of which become system building blocks.

- Provides one integrated product for IT security and physical access control.
- Enables current and future compatibility with biometric, software, and security standards.

A self-developing system: developers of biometric technologies and security systems databases will never stop advancing their solutions, all of which are system's building blocks.

All of the above advantages of the novel solution would assist a financial company in incorporating such system to curtail the problem of fraud. Further, different financial organizations can build and utilize a single biometric security system without sharing any of their confidential or other sensitive information, because only the biometric information is stored in the system. Thus, a significant economy of scale can be realized without compromising any sensitive information. Any internal security and other applications can be integrated into the system with minimal time and effort and without unnecessary optimization, testing and quality control. In other words, the new system offers building blocks for a customizable and self-evolving system utilizing modular construction and interoperability.

Thus, the following benefits can be realized:

- *Minimization of costs and time for development, management, support and training.*
- *Elimination of fraud cases and associated savings from not having to deal with its consequences.*
- *Protection of customer information by not sharing it between financial organizations, dispelling privacy concerns.*
- *Individualized biometric solutions for all users (customers and employees), regardless of the different identification needs of different departments.*
- *Easy and fast integration of any new third-party application using secure biometrics.*

Chapter Seven

Assurance Standards for the Consumer Identity Ecosystem

Andrew Nash and Brett McDowell, PayPal with special thanks to Brett Glade, "RSA, The Security Division of EMC"

Thesis

THE challenges of Internet commerce and banking grow daily. Unlike zero or low-value transaction environments such as social networking, the impact of failing to successfully establish the identities of participants in high-value transactions has direct business impact with the potential to cripple the unwary. Any significant increase in the number of basis points of fraud loss directly impacts the profitability of our businesses. Exposure of private consumer information threatens our brands. In some cases, we merely look foolish or incompetent. In other more extreme failures, regulators may levy significant fines or even remove the licenses we need to carry on our businesses. At the same time, we are under pressure to be compliant with an ever-increasing number of domestic and international regulations, not to mention the ever-present need to grow and realize new business opportunities at the same time.

In response to the risk factors, we continue to build ever more sophisticated fraud/risk evaluation models. From a compliance standpoint, we roll out new technologies to help us track and audit transactions and activity. We work with our business and product teams to help innovate, trying to balance the business needs with the sensitive security systems we have in place. Information is constantly gleaned about consumers and used for many purposes, including but not limited to:

- Continuous feedback biometrics
- Historical analysis of Internet presence and existence or transaction patterns
- Correlation of dynamic information including geo-location
- Routing paths
- Blacklists of known pockets of Internet "badness"

And the list goes on. All the while, we struggle with the consumer experience this may present. For all of us, the true "F-word" to avoid is friction.

Now more than ever, we are in need of sources of trusted identities that can help distinguish how much information gathering and analysis -- pain and friction from the consumer's perspective -- to subject our customers to as we balance risk and compliance factors with the pursuit of new business. Whether as smaller businesses primarily relying on identities verified by others or as larger entities actually in the business of vetting identities and protecting customer information, there is a need for a consumer identity ecosystem that uses a common language of evaluation so we all have a shared understanding of assurance in the assertions of identity that we rely upon.

The need for a standards-based consumer identity ecosystem is not unique to financial services. Many diverse industries and governments have also identified this requirement and have successfully collaborated over a number of years to deliver an open standard to meet this very need, the Kantara Initiative Identity Assurance Framework (IAF). The IAF is the product of a consolidation between the American government–initiated E-Authentication Partnership (EAP) and the industry-initiated Liberty Alliance Project (LAP). The IAF standard and certification program is now under the stewardship of Kantara Initiative, an open public-private consortium launched as a consolidation of industry groups in 2009. Kantara Initiative representatives worked in coordination with Federal CIO Council representatives to further refine the IAF to meet the Obama administration's requirements for their Open Identity Solutions for Open Government program (OISOG). The result of this broad consolidation and public-private collaboration is IAF 2.0[1], a Kantara Initiative Recommendation recognized by the US federal government as an approved Trust Framework under the OISOG program[2]

This rapid development in government and industry demands, coupled with unprecedented consumer connectivity, are factors that have forever changed the questions we've been asking ourselves in the financial services industry. It's no longer relevant to engage in yesterday's debate of when, where, or if we will develop a common standard for enabling trust between consumers of our services over the Internet. The question we must ask ourselves today is simply, "What role are we each going to play within this redefined cross-industry, open, standards-based consumer identity ecosystem?"

The Financial Services Context

It is hardly surprising that financial institutions have been one of the market segments most concerned about identification, identities, authentication, access control, and the various other procedural, operational, and technical aspects of establishing who their customers are. Compliance and other regulatory pressures are an artifact demonstrating that various governments and governing bodies also recognize that, for the industry to be successful, consumers and enterprises to be protected, the financing of terrorism to be diminished, governments to collect taxes due to them, and the institutions themselves not to be defrauded, knowing who your customer is with a high degree of certainty is critical.

Early days of banking relied on face-to-face relationships to establish knowledge of consumers. Relationship establishment required presentation of sufficient proofs and then a history of interactions to establish a level of trust that was the basis of future transactions. Banks and other letters of credit or introduction served to establish a network of relationships outside of local areas to facilitate wider commercial and financial transactions and travel[3].

The introduction of electronic forms of commercial and financial interactions has always built on various analogs of the earliest forms of identity proof and trust establishment. The problems inherent in electronic interactions are well understood, and most attempts to provide an equivalent to local knowledge

---

[1] http://kantarainitiative.org/confluence/display/GI/Identity+Assurance+Framework+v2.0

[2] http://www.idmanagement.gov/

[3] http://infodagang2u.blogspot.com/2007/11/history-of-letter-of-credit.html

and individual recognition have been struggling to provide adequate solutions ever since the emergence of the telegraph. Electronic funds transfer mechanisms, automatic bank tellers, extension of payment terminals into commercial entities, electronic inter-bank transfers, credit cards, and, finally, Internet commerce have created an environment where we are always running to catch up with the implications and new emerging threats associated with the updated technologies.

In commercial and financial transactions, certainty exists only in the minds of the uninformed. Whether dealing with errors, misunderstandings, theft, or other forms of deliberate subversion, all entities must make allowance for loss due to fraud and other risks. The challenge is that the cost of this loss is directly seen at the bottom line, and profitability suffers as a result. Allocations to cover losses in this area are substantial, and the number of basis points of losses is carefully watched. Generally, the fine-grain details are a highly guarded secret in enterprises and financial institutions.

Today, with the majority of the world population interacting via the Internet and the distance between entities that can establish identity and trust being stretched to the limit, the risk of fraud inherent in this expanding ecosystem is causing accelerated strain and challenges at all levels. The sheer scale of the problem, coupled with unprecedented connectivity, the low cost of perpetrating fraud, and the even lower likelihood of criminals being prosecuted, all compound the issues.

The fundamental issues remain the same and are independent of the technologies:

- How do you establish the identities of the participants in a transaction?
- How much trust can you place on them?
- How much corresponding risk are you going to assume?

This would be difficult enough if it were not also complicated by considering the amount worth expending to achieve a sufficient level of trust for a given category of transaction. Generally, the decision to engage in this expanding

ecosystem comes down to a cost/benefit analysis based on the value of the transaction, the associated risks, and the cost of mitigating those risks. In some cases,
the calculations are informed by various regulations that require minimum standards be applied.

Inter-bank transactions are a reasonably tractable problem. The total transaction value tends to be very large and the number of participants relatively
small, at least compared to the problem of identifying consumers transacting via
the Internet. Many inter-bank protocols and transactions have been successfully
implemented over the years. Some, like the Automated Clearinghouse (ACH)
network, have continued to adapt as technology shifts.

We all must deal with two fundamentally different classes of identification in this ever-expanding payments ecosystem. The first is, by comparison,
simple. A financial institution needs to identify its own customers to facilitate
direct interactions for account management or other transactions within the
institution itself, e.g. account management. The other class is how to identify
other institutions' customers when they present themselves to us or our own
customers as they present themselves at another institution or enterprise, i.e.
cross-organizational transactions. Various attempts have been made to facilitate
identification of consumers between financial institutions, who are, of course,
only a small subset of the payments ecosystem, especially at today's Internet scale.
Most have been enormously costly and generally failed to meet expectations. In
some cases, this was due to the complexity of the technologies used, e.g Public
Key Infrastructure (PKI)[4]. In others, the problems lay in the organizational and
procedural complexity and overhead. IdenTrust[5] is perhaps the example most
familiar to industry stakeholders as an example of a costly infrastructure with low
utility at Internet scale.

The real problem remains in the scale of the Internet, given the number of
consumers that need to be identified within transactions. Sheer volume strains our
confidence, our trust and risk evaluations become more difficult, and we eventually find that classical methods fail us. As a result, progressively, there has been
a trend away from strict identification and guarantees to risk-based evaluation
techniques[6]. The cost to the participants in the transaction flow and the impact
on consumers remain a problem that we struggle to address. Methodologies in

---

[4] http://en.wikipedia.org/wiki/Public_key_infrastructure
[5] http://identrust.com/
[6] http://www.ffiec.gov/pdf/authentication_guidance.pdf

this area are tending to move from detailed analysis of all consumers to quickly identifying the good guys and then passing them through as gently as possible while still scrutinizing the suspects with ever more powerful heuristic and correlation models.

The Open Approach: Collaboration, Transparency, and Consolidation of Effort

What we need is a fundamentally new approach to the problem. The status quo is unsustainable. If the all-too-familiar data breach headline or the increasingly negative-trending government and NGO reports[7] on the state of identity fraud, with increased regulatory pressure as a result, are any sign of our industry's health, the forecast would aptly be described as death by a thousand paper cuts. While our line managers have had no choice but to stanch this bleeding with more and more bandages, those of us with a strategic mandate have been focused on what can be done about the infrastructure underpinning our ecosystem. How can we attack the problem at its source and meet compliance issues and new business opportunities at a systemic level that will bring about game-changing results? Well, it is only logical that tackling a systemic problem in any ecosystem like ours, with inherent dependencies on the actions of numerous industry and government stakeholders, would start with a collaboration of those stakeholders. Then why is it our industry has continued to attempt to solve this problem within our industry alone or, worse yet, as individual companies? It's no wonder we've had so many false starts over the years[8][9][10][11].

The problem isn't within the financial services infrastructure itself, but buried deep within the consumer identity ecosystem our payment channels depend upon. The problem is not a technology problem. It's a common sense problem. We are collectively engaged in an Internet-scale shell game of overwhelming complexity that we have somehow deluded ourselves into expecting the consumer will manage in an enlightened, disciplined, and consistent manner simply because it's in her self-interest to do so. How many online accounts does

---

[7] http://www.idtheftcenter.org/artman2/publish/lib_survey/index.shtml

[8] http://www.symantec.com/press/2004/n041117b.html

[9] http://www.fstc.org/press/press_detail.php?id=56

[10] http://www.fstc.org/projects/index.php?id=23

[11] http://www.fdic.gov/consumers/consumer/idtheftstudy/industry.html

your average customer have? How many different enrollment processes has she been asked to endure? How many credentials (user name/passwords pairs, second-factor photographs, or other forms of authentication credential) does she have to establish and manage? Given this worsening situation for consumers, why do we delude ourselves in expecting them to comply with high-friction recommendations such as:

1) Order copies of your credit report routinely to ensure accuracy.
2) Don't pay your bills from your own mailbox.
3) Cover your hand when entering your PIN at an ATM.
4) Never provide personal or credit card information over the phone unless you initiated the call
5) Use a different, strong password at every site on the Internet you do business with

Yes, these recommendations are commonsense and would help. But do we really expect consumers follow them -- do you? The status quo of putting the onus on the consumer to manage cyber-security best practices creates more friction and is rapidly approaching its expiration date with policy makers as evident by the National Strategy for Trusted Identities in Cyberspace (NSTIC) which has at its core the creation and maintenance of a high-assurance, privacy-respecting opt-in government sanctioned Identity Ecosystem[12]. Given its pedigree and status as an approved Trust Framework for Levels of Assurance 1 through 3, the IAF is perfectly positioned as the foundation for this emerging Identity Ecosystem as defined in The NSTIC.

Many organizations besides the US Federal Government are turning to the IAF[13] -- deployed in conjunction with open standards-based federated identity technologies like OpenID[14], Information Cards[15], Security Assertion Markup

---

[12] http://www.whitehouse.gov/blog/2010/06/25/national-strategy-trusted-identities-cyberspace

[13] http://kantarainitiative.org/wordpress/programs/assurance-certification/

[14] http://openid.net/developers/specs/

[15] http://docs.oasis-open.org/imi/identity/v1.0/os/identity-1.0-spec-os.html

Language (SAML)[16], and OAuth[17] -- to get in front of this trend and find ways to:

- Reduce our risk and compliance overhead
- Reduce friction for our customers
- Enhance our customer's experience with our branded services
- Better protect our organizations from fraud losses

An IAF-enabled consumer identity ecosystem is an opportunity to change the game in fundamental ways that improve consumer experience on the Internet and the associated business offerings you can reach them with, help to meet compliance demands (privacy in particular), and reduce risk to identity-based fraud. As a game-changing innovation, the IAF is both an opportunity and a threat for your business. To understand which side of that proposition you stand on, you must first understand how the IAF works with federated identity technologies.

The Identity Trust Gradient

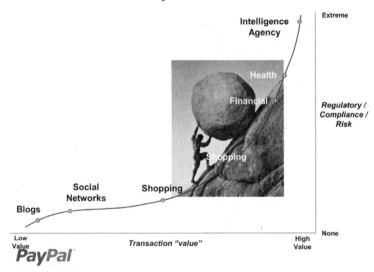

---

[16] http://docs.oasis-open.org/security/saml/v2.0/sstc-saml-approved-errata-2.0.html

[17] https://datatracker.ietf.org/doc/draft-ietf-oauth-v2/

As the value of a transaction increases in terms of money, reputation, IP involved, and so forth, the importance of protecting that transaction naturally increases. But how do we uniformly evaluate that trust? And how can or should we share those trust metrics with our partners, affiliates, and so forth as we strive to reduce friction, simplify the customer experience, and achieve goals toward delivering new business offerings?

This is where the IAF comes into play. The IAF defines a few key roles[18] for transactions in the new consumer identity ecosystem:

Credential service provider (CSP): An electronic trust service provider that operates one or more credential services[19]. e.g. your workplace network administrator, your social networking service , a government entity, your financial institution, etc.

Relying party (RP): An entity that relies upon a subscriber's credentials, typically to process a transaction or grant access to information or a system e.g. a retailer relying on a payment service provider to assert the identity of the customer to fulfill the transaction.

Subscriber: A party that has entered into an agreement to use an electronic trust service, e.g. your customer who is either using your service as their CSP or someone else as CSP and authenticating to you in your role as the RP in that transaction.

The IAF is about business operations, not technology choices. The end goal of the IAF is to provide public and private sector organizations with a uniform means of relying on electronic credentials issued by a variety of CSP's in order to reduce friction in the consumer's online experience while simultaneously reducing risk and clarifying liability between all parties in the transaction..

---

[18] http://kantarainitiative.org/confluence/download/attachments/41649275/Kantara+IAF-1100-Glossary.pdf

[19] Credential Service: A type of electronic trust service that supports the verification of identities (identity proofing), the issuance of identity related assertions/credentials/tokens, and the subsequent management of those credentials (for example, renewal, revocation, and the provision of related status and authentication services).

Since you understand how ATMs work, you already understand the basic tenants and benefits of a federated approach:

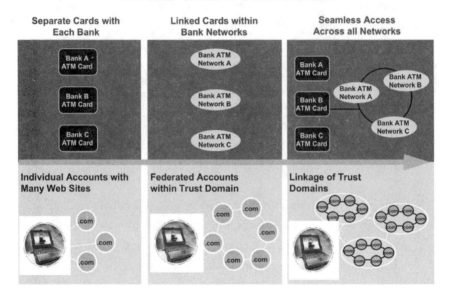

ATMs and Federation

The IAF provides a means to enable relying parties to understand the trustworthiness of electronic identity credentials by other parties at one of four commonly agreed levels of assurance (LOA)[20] by standardizing criteria for the processes and procedures CSP's must follow in order to be certified at the appropriate LOA. The IAF specifies the verification and proofing checks that CSPs carry out on subscribers, the way that CSPs run the security-related aspects of their services, and how the CSPs themselves are assessed to verify they are operating their business in conformance with their proclaimed level(s) of assurance and their stated terms of service. Kantara Initiative accredits assessors that then may be hired by a CSP to perform assessments of their credential service. Once the assessment is complete an attestation is provided to the Kantara Initiative Assurance Review Board who then issues a Kantara Initiative Certified™ trustmark, making all results publicly available so RP's know which CSP's have been

---

[20] The IAF references the guidance provided by the United States National Institute of Standards and Technology (NIST) Special Publication 800-63, which outlines four levels of assurance, ranging in confidence level from 1=low to 4=very high.

certified to what LOA[21]. With a widely recognized LOA model, government endorsement, and a public-private consortia providing accredited assessors and service certifications at all levels of assurance, it's time for the financial services industry to embrace this cross-industry program as its own and begin both deploying and consuming certified commercial credential services to reduce customer friction and risk of fraud.

Conclusions

Internet commerce represents both a huge opportunity and a huge risk to all of us. That is not news. The use of the Internet continues to skyrocket for all types of transactions, and the level of value of those transactions is increasing. This is also not news. What is news is we now have the IAF, the OISOG government initiative, the Kantara Initiative as a collaboration forum and certification authority, and the White House NSTIC calling on us to collaboratively deliver a trustworthy Identity Ecosystem to the Nation that will help solve many of the problems we have been facing heretofore on our own. Now is the time to finally embrace the four LOA model for valuing the level of risk and associated trust of our transactions and throw the market power of our industry behind the Identity Ecosystem initiative. We have the tools and the political will upgrade our infrastructure and practices to reduce our risks and the friction our customers encounter as they perform transactions electronically. The parade has started and whether we like it or not, we are the industry out in front. We can either start marching and maintain our leadership position as trusted stewards of high-value personal information or we can stand still and get run over.

Suggested Sidebar

The IAF and its basic tenants of consistent trust analysis and valuation are already returning benefits in industry. A January 2009 profile from International Data Corporatoin (IDC), "Citi Capitalizes on Identity Framework and Standards for Its Global Transactions Services," details how Citi is using common frameworks and practices with customers to reduce friction, achieve compliance, reduce costs, and achieve new business offerings.

According to Citi, clients in the pharmaceuticals space are seeing six- to

---

[21] http://kantarainitiative.org/wordpress/programs/assurance-certification/

seven-digit hard dollar savings per year. In the ROI, some include saving more than two tons of printed (and sometimes notarized) paper per year. Other benefits, such as a reduction of costs related to IP losses and reduction in the overall R&D timeline, will be proven in due time.

Citi is looking to build on its success and expand the model into other industries. The company believes there are additional drivers in this market, beyond cost savings, compliance, and risk. Noting that all these are typically associated with the "stick" as opposed to the "carrot" approach, Citi emphasizes that all of these initiatives must be implemented with scalability in mind. New industry initiatives revolve around the "go green" theme. With senior management teams being asked to show measurable results in implementing environmentally conscious initiatives, eliminating paper-intensive processes is one popular choice. Another market driver is the ability to increase operational capacity by automating and removing manual steps, for example, in financial processes such as loans and the supply chain. Finally, at the end of the day, making the service more secure and convenient is a differentiation to which customers attribute significant value.

IDC offered this *Advice for Buyers* with regards to the IAF and this approach. *"The time is now to take action on this, especially in financial services. The end results will be increased compliance and cost efficiency, which is needed to increase revenue and margins."*

The profile contained this advice to other providers. *"Citi's approach to digital assurance has caught many by surprise: banks are expected to focus on the banking business, not the IT or information security business, that's only for technology companies. The reality is that digital identity is more of a risk management issue than it is a technological issue, and hence the natural fit for a bank. Customers are starting to catch up with this notion."*

"Citi emphatically believes that standards are essential to a successful implementation, even at the cost of a slower time to market. The advice to vendors: buyers truly value open and interoperable standards when making vendor decisions."

Special thanks to IDC for allowing reprint of the italicized portion. A full copy of the profile is available at www.idc.com

CHAPTER EIGHT

HOW IS ACH BEING ATTACKED AND WHAT CAN YOU DO

MIKE MULHOLAND, MEMENTO INC

THE impetus for the development of the ACH system was the American government's desire to reduce the number of paper checks being generated not only by the government itself, but by commercial issuers as well. The model was that of an ongoing recurring payment relationship between two known parties. This system met the objectives of the government by producing a secure and inexpensive mechanism for processing payments between government and business entities and private persons. The low risk associated with the system had much to do with the relationship between the parties.

The introduction of nonrecurring payment types initially allowed for conversion of checks into ACH transactions and then remote approval of ACH debits to the receiver's account. This allowed for a fundamental shift in the relationship between the parties of the transaction from an ongoing recurring payment relationship between two known parties to a onetime payment between two parties who didn't necessarily know each other, even though they may have had a transaction in the past.

While this type of payment is intrinsically more risky than the traditional ACH payment, the fraud that was predicted by some hasn't been evidenced in the numbers as expected. So why is this? If more risk is being introduced through the nature of the new transaction types, where is the accompanying increase in fraud? An analysis of ACH activity shows an interesting thing. Looking at 2008 data, we find the nonrecurring transaction types are being used predominantly to initiate repeating onetime transactions. Accounts Receivable Entry (ARC),

Internet-Initiated Entry (WEB), and Telephone-Initiated Entry (TEL), the three predominant nonrecurring transaction types volume-wise, are used overwhelmingly for initiation of bill pay transactions. (96.3 percent, 90.3 percent, and 88.6 percent, respectively).[1] This is significant because these repeating onetime transactions display similar relationship characteristics as the traditional ACH transaction, that of an ongoing repeating (as opposed to recurring) payment relationship between two known parties. If the premise that the risk in the ACH is based largely (though not entirely) on the underlying relationship between the parties of the transaction is true, then the lack of a smoking gun is not surprising. Less than 6 percent of ACH transactions represent a truly onetime payment relationship between two parties who may not know each other in the same sense as the traditional ACH relationship.

Before we are lulled into a false sense of security though, we should recognize a few things:

- The percentage of higher risk transactions will inevitably grow. An increase in electronic transactions will offset the continuing decline in check transactions. Clearly, debit card has been a big beneficiary of that trend, but so has ACH, and this will continue. There are also a number of new players in the ACH world, alternative payments mechanisms if you will. These will drive additional ACH volume, predominately falling in that riskier category.

- Originally, a relative few actually had access to the ACH channel. That access is broadening rapidly with an expanding array of ways to initiate an ACH transaction, primarily through online banking, including mobile. This is another significant change in the underlying structure of ACH, and increased access translates to increased risk.

- There is not a good way to verify ownership of an account being used for a transaction. Banks and other players began using microcredits to test accounts involved in transfers and funding transactions, but this technique only shows access to an account, not ownership. While it's true that access equals ownership for legitimate transactions, we are only kidding ourselves if we believe this is an effective deterrent for fraud.

We should also keep in mind that there have always been ways to perpetrate fraud in the ACH channel, new transaction types notwithstanding.

The Attacks

The ACH system can be attacked in a number of ways by multiple fraudsters, including first parties, insiders, and third parties. Some of the schemes have existed for years, and some are made possible by changes in the way ACH system is accessed and used. We will discuss each attack vector in turn and identify the type of fraud and the perpetrator.

Invalid debit origination occurs as first-party fraud. This fraud involves an originator who generates invalid debits and then continues to generate more debits to cover returns as they start to come in. Eventually, they drain the account associated with the ACH origination activities and abscond with as much money as they can. This is a financial game of chicken where the fraudster tries to judge when the bank will shut him down for excessive returns and takes the money and runs as close to that point as he is comfortable with. This is not a new scheme. I heard my first example of it around 1984 involving college students to the tune of around two million dollars.

Insider fraud is another first-party fraud where invalid debits and credits can be generated. Here, an insider at the company or the bank modifies existing transactions or adds new transactions to a file. Committing this fraud via credit transactions is straightforward. The fraudster simply modifies existing credits in an outgoing file or adds new credits to receiver accounts he, an accomplice, or a money mule controls. Debits can be used as well by making the fraudster's account one of the offsetting accounts used in a debit origination file. This version, of course, is only possible if the company presents a balanced file, which contains the offsets, to the ODFI . (Originating Depository Financial Institution). The file itself could have invalid debits in it as well. This may be done so the offset amounts to the company's normal offset account are the expected amounts. A bank insider can also manipulate the files by making sure they adjust the hash totals in the control records so the file remains balanced.

Kiting is perpetrated by first parties that can be put into three groups:

- The accidental kiter who kites through poor bookkeeping or error is generally not a problem and generally corrects the situation as soon as he is told of it.

- The situational kiter, or cash flow kiter, knowingly and purposefully kites to resolve a temporary cash flow shortfall. Obviously more dangerous because of willful intent, many look upon this kiter somewhat benignly.
- Clearly the most dangerous is the purposeful kiter. While certainly not as prevalent as the cash flow kiter, these are the guys who can generate millions in losses.

A big problem with kiting behavior that is often overlooked is that kiting is a slippery slope. The accidental kiter becomes a cash flow kiter, and the cash flow kiter gets in too deep and becomes a purposeful kiter.

Kiting can be accomplished via ACH transactions in two ways:

- The first is a special case of the invalid debit origination scheme described above. Here, the kiter is relying on return float, which can actually be many times longer than clearing float. He may use a past customer whose information is still in accounts receivable, an account number he got from an external source, or an accomplice. He knows the debit is coming back, but, by that time, he will be out of his cash crunch, and he can explain it away as an error. In the worst case, he can generate another debit to cover the first debit's return.
- The second is a classic round-robin kite scheme. Think of it as an electronic version of a paper-based kite scheme. Because settlement times are very predictable in ACH, the kiter knows exactly when he will have to cover his kiting transactions. Either credits or debits can be used in these schemes, but debits are more popular because the credit scheme can be stopped by simply requiring good funds before file origination. In a simple round-robin, A sends a debit to B, who sends a debit to C, who sends a debit to A. The credit offset of each of these outgoing debits covers the incoming debit.

Penny credit is a first-party fraud scheme that is used for data gathering. It relies on the practice of sending challenge deposits to verify valid accounts. The fraudster adds micro-credits to an existing file or generates a file of micro-credits. These generally target a specific bank or banks and use the account number structure of that bank with the last three or four digits being incremental. Every account number associated with a transaction that is returned is discarded. The remainders make up a valid account list to be sold or used by the perpetrator for additional fraudulent activity.

Invalid debit or counterfeit ACH is an attack by a third party against the true originator. Invalid debits are generated by providing an account number that a secondary victim owns to the originator. The originator processes the transactions in good faith, only to see them returned up to sixty or even ninety days later. Even when the merchant generates a test credit, the fraudster can provide the needed verification in an account takeover or friendly fraud situation.

The concept of primary and secondary victim applies here because the fraud is perpetrated against the originator, who will exchange something of value with the fraudster while the secondary victim's account is debited for the amount of the fraud. The originator is the primary victim because he warrants that all of the ACH transactions he originates are valid. The secondary victim has sixty days from the settlement date of the transaction to return an unauthorized transaction and sixty days from the statement date showing that transaction to register a Regulation E claim. Even though the secondary victim can usually recover the stolen funds, there may be other undesirable effects, such as an overdrawn account, returned items, fees, and negative status with creditors and merchants. Invalid debits can also be generated by negotiating a counterfeit check, which is then converted into a counterfeit ACH item.

Origination system hijacking occurs when a third-party fraudster initiates invalid ACH transactions in the name of the true originator or initiator. In today's world of online access to Web-based origination applications, online fraud facilitates the ACH fraud. The fraudster compromises the credentials of an individual who has access to the origination system or online banking system and generates transactions as him. It is a form of identity theft. It is clear that the nexus between information security, especially online security, and fraud continues to become more significant. There are two categories of origination system hijacking: commercial and retail. In all cases, the hijacker uses a variety of methods from phishing, keyloggers and other Trojans, or man-in-the-middle attacks to compromise the victim's credentials. Once the victim's credentials have been compromised, the fraudster is essentially the victim from an online perspective.

In the commercial world, the victim is an originator, so the fraudster uses the origination system to originate items as the originator. These will be credit files that may mimic some characteristic of the originator's normal credit files in order to disguise them. They may also make no attempt to disguise the transactions they are originating and simply extract as much money as they can as quickly as possible. Once credentials are compromised, it is a very simple and straightforward, but effective, scheme. This is the scheme that got everyone's attention in 2009 with an estimated one hundred and twenty million dollars in perpetrations from this single scheme.

In the retail environment, the fraudster is attacking a slightly different target in that while the victim is technically the originator, they do not have access to the origination system and act as the initiator of the transaction. The defacto originator in this case is the bank providing the online banking services. The fraudster is attacking the online banking system that is the front end for the origination system, so to speak. The fraudster compromises the credentials of the retail customer as described above and accesses the online banking system as the customer. There follows a series of steps, some of which may occur in the commercial account take-over described above as well:
:
- He can scout the customer's relationship, identifying accounts, balances, and banking products used, especially bill pay and transfer capabilities.
- The fraudster may set the victim up for services he doesn't currently use that will allow the fraudster to more easily extract funds from the victim's account(s).
- The bank is prevented from effectively communicating with the customer. Because banks often provide alerts and notices via e-mail or text messages, the fraudster will change the e-mail address slightly and/or the mobile device number. This will prevent the customer from becoming immediately aware of strange transactions on his accounts.
- The fraudster may then consolidate funds from other accounts into the DDA through online-initiated internal transfers.
- Finally, funds are extracted through an online banking transaction that is often executed through the ACH.

This can happen over a period of several days or in as little as one or two days depending on the capabilities and policies of the bank's online banking system.

The fraudster owns or controls the accounts the credits are sent to, and they are emptied upon receipt of the credit. Unwitting, albeit gullible, mules are sometimes used. The possibility of friendly fraud (fraud committed by someone known to the victim who may have or easily gain access to credentials) or collusion on the part of the victim should not be discounted in this type of fraud.

Reverse phishing is a particularly innovative third-party fraud scheme. So dubbed because it is facilitated through communication to the victim, but, rather than soliciting information, it provides information and instructions to follow. The fraudster contacts a victim who generates ACH credits to pay his trading partner(s). The communication, for example, an e-mail spoofed to appear to be coming from the real trading partner, instructs the victim to send his remittance to a new account. The victim complies with this request without verifying its authenticity. The fraudster who absconds with the funds, of course, controls the new account. The trading partner sends the victim a past-due notice (usually the first one at thirty days), and the fraud is discovered. The victim is liable for the loss because he made a change to his payment arrangements without proper authorization. Corrections are made, the trading partner is paid, and the victim is left stunned. The possibility of insider involvement either in the victim organization or the trading partner should be considered.

The Defense

Defenses against the ACH attack vectors described above share commonalities, but also have some unique properties depending on the fraud scheme. Some are, by necessity, more proactive than others are, but all require understanding the nature of the transactions contained in the files being processed as well as the circumstances under which the items are being generated. The majority of the detection techniques described here are on the ODFI side, which is logical because that's where the risk lies, but there are techniques for the RDFI (Receiving Depository Financial Institution) as well.

Detection involves transaction monitoring and applying analytics and logical tools to root out the small percentage of fraudulent transactions in a sea of valid ones. In order to successfully do this, we need to take a more comprehensive view of the operating environment of our originators and receivers. The transactions themselves are not enough. We must develop a contextual view of the transaction flow by considering other related information. Think of the valid transactions as being part of a payments ecosystem so to speak. In order to identify the foreign object, for example, fraudulent transaction, you must understand the ecosystem. Monitoring involves identifying behavior that is out of character for the originator or receiver. While many fraudulent items will be unusual, not all unusual items will be fraud, and some normal-looking items will be fraudulent. This is the conundrum for those who monitor on too narrow of a view of the transaction, a single facet if you will. Transactions, like diamonds, are multifaceted. The contextual view of the account includes everything that is happening to it, not just a narrow view of the transactions being monitored.

Monitoring also involves recognizing characteristic patterns of events. Just as completion of banking transactions has a process, so does the perpetration of a fraud as well. The more complex the scheme, the more steps there are, and the longer it takes to perpetrate. Identify the processes by analyzing losses from the standpoint of the perpetration process and be able to monitor for and identify it when it occurs again. The fraudster needs access and information in order to perpetrate the fraud, and every action he takes leaves a trace, an electronic signature so to speak. The key is to find those telltale bits of evidence before the fraudulent movement of funds.

ODFI Monitoring

For the ODFI, monitor the characteristics of the origination and the context in which it takes place. Things you want to be aware of are:

- **Access from an unusual location.** Is the access from a different IP address or machine ID than the user normally uses? A really sophisticated fraudster can defeat this through spoofing or, worse yet, making a bot slave of the victim's PC, but it's a good first check.
- **Unusual inquiry activity.** Look for patterns of inquiry the customer would normally not do. The fraudster is on a reconnaissance mission to discover the particulars of the account relationship.
- **Unusual origination system activity.** When the fraudster is testing the waters, he may test functionality, such as create a file and delete it or access a script or template, modify it, and then delete the modified script.
- **Unusual maintenance activity.** Especially look for changes in contact information (e-mail and/or cell number), change to existing product, or new product setup.

- **Out-of-pattern originations (or initiations on the retail side).**

    - Look at time of month, day of week, or time of day: This could be in general or specific to a particular file type or receiver set.
    - Look at file makeup. This could be number of items, total dollar amount, or average dollar amount per item.
    - Look at unusual receivers. Are there first-time receivers? Is the file made up entirely of first-time receivers? Is there anything else unusual about the receivers?
    - Look at unusual SEC code use. Are the SEC codes consistent with the customer's agreed upon or historical use of the ACH?
    - Look at list checking. This could be blocks and filters. At the account level, it could be accepted SEC codes or list of accepted receivers.

- Look at ACH Positive Pay: This is essentially a pre-notification to the bank via a different channel of items that are going to be originated, especially credits.

RDFI Monitoring

The RDFI monitoring for retail accounts is often viewed as a customer service–oriented activity rather than loss prevention because of the sixty-day return schedule for unauthorized. We should all keep in mind that posting unexpected and unauthorized transactions to an account could have serious negative ramifications other than a loss on that item. For commercial accounts, the sixty-day return schedule and Regulation E do not apply, so timely review is much more critical. RDFI monitoring can be done at both the bank level and the account level. Things to look for include

- A large number of items from a new originator or sudden change in volume from a known originator (bank level)
- A high return rate to a particular originator (bank level)
- Unusual items for an account (especially debits)

    - Originator: First-time, risky, or unusual originators
    - Timing: Doesn't fit with usual ACH receiving pattern
    - Dollar amount: An unusually high- or out-of-pattern dollar amount

- Nonrecurring: Most ACH items are recurring. Non-recurring items are riskier.

- A new account whose first ACH credit is from a non-commercial originator, for example, the originator is a bank (bill pay), and/or a CIE entry class code is used. This is looking for mule accounts.
- List checking. This could be blocks and filters. At the account level, it could be accepted SEC codes or list of accepted originators. It could include blacklists of known bad or risky originators.
- ACH Positive Pay. This is essentially pre-notification to the bank of expected ACH debits

The Prevention

Mitigation is all about putting yourself into a position where it is difficult to perpetrate the fraud. Identify and eliminate the vulnerabilities inherent in your processes and products. Learn from your experience. Every loss you take is the result of some identifiable scheme. Understand them, identify the techniques used to attack you, and take steps to stop them by eliminating the vulnerabilities that are being exploited. Or, at the very least, become aware of those vulnerabilities in your detection strategies.

Here are general mitigation steps, many of which we have heard before. Most of which will seem like commonsense sorts of things that are sometimes overlooked. A number of general steps that apply to any ACH product or process and others are specific to a fraud scheme or an ACH-based product.

- Education and awareness is very important in reducing vulnerabilities. Educate your originators not only about how a product works, but also about how fraudsters could attack the product. General education about online security is also critical as access to the payments system moves more and more toward the electronic methodologies. Bank staff needs to be educated about attack vectors and how to recognize possible fraud perpetration and practices and activity that increase vulnerability. Many frauds are successfully perpetrated because of a breakdown in or circumvention of controls.
- Due diligence is absolutely essential for stopping fraud before it gets under way. Know your originator. The due diligence should be as

robust as that used for a credit decision. Also keep track of originators who have been terminated and applicants that have been rejected. They may turn up again under a different guise.

- Basic blocking and tackling is important. Everyone says monitor your accounts, and it makes perfect sense to do so. Yet it's amazing to see the number of customers who just don't do it regularly.

- Wherever possible, require unbalanced file submission. The bank will generate the offsets through some prearranged procedure.

- Separation of duties is an important safeguard that should be required for all originators. The same person should not do origination and reconcilement, for example. The origination and release process could be separate processes that engage multiple people at the company. Proactive activities should be in a separate channel as well. For example, the person who creates or releases the file should not be the one who provides the bank with acceptable recipients or offset accounts.

- Work with your third-party processors. Make sure their due diligence processes meet your standards. Help them develop a due diligence plan and process. Always maintain the right of refusal for existing originators as well as for new applicants.

- Blocks and filters can be used very effectively on a case-by-case basis. They can range from acceptable SEC codes to acceptable originators to acceptable receivers to a full ACH Positive Pay where the customer forewarns the bank of expected ACH debits or provides an issue file through a different channel prior to an ACH origination.

- Work closely with our originators. Monitor return rates for each originator to identify when a particular originator may be under attack through invalid debit origination schemes. Help them develop methods to protect themselves better from these attacks.

- Make sure you integrate your fraud detection systems to help detect cross-channel fraud, especially in the area of ACH check conversions.

- Kite scenarios usually start in positive territory and go negative over time. The majority of kiters are situational kiters, those who kite for a short time to cover a short cash flow. These kiters in particular will display risky behavior before they start kiting. At best, a kite is an unnegotiated, unsecured loan. The bank and the customer would be far better off addressing the problem that underlies the kiting behavior.

By offering overdraft protection or a cash flow revolving credit, you can proactively resolve the customer's problem and strengthen the relationship as well as apply credit-based controls and create new revenue.

- Profit from your experience by developing lists of known fraud information such as known bad receivers, known bad IP addresses, and other fraud data that can be used in blacklists.
- Develop a list of acceptable penny originators so you can use it in screening both originators sending to you and your own originators. ODFIs should quickly investigate this activity.
- For online banking, start with the customer. You are granting him access to your network. Make sure he is a responsible user of that network and a good steward of the trust you inherently give him. Develop and use best practices for IT security and your online interaction with your customer. Educate him about the risks and vulnerabilities connected with the Internet. Just as you require him to meet certain technical requirements to gain access to your network, include security measures in those requirements.
- In the case of reverse phishing, an ounce of prevention is worth way more than a pound of cure. Customers should independently verify any instructions for changes in remittance arrangements. Do not use the same communications channel for verification. For example, don't just reply to the e-mail requesting verification. Deal with someone you know at the company to verify.

1. National Automated Clearinghouse Association (NACHA)

CHAPTER NINE

SMART CARDS

RANDY VANDERHOOF, SMART CARD ALLIANCE

Smart Card History and Market

A smart card (integrated circuit card) is a device in which an integrated circuit or chip is embedded. The development of smart cards dates back to the 1970s when patents were filed in France, Germany, and Japan. The first practical smart card implementation was in France to combat the rising cost of fraud in telecommunications and banking applications. Motorola produced the first secure single-chip microcontroller (MCU) in 1979 for use in French bank cards. Two types of smart card products were introduced in the early 1980s. One, for telephone cards, used a serial-memory integrated circuit (IC). The other, for banking applications, used the more secure MCU.

The first mass rollout of smart cards took place in 1992 when all French banks adopted the cards. More than ten million cards were issued that year. MCU smart card shipments have grown dramatically, with 4.520 billion shipped in 2009[22] and over 4.995 billion expected to ship in 2010. This rapid growth is due to the increasing use of smart cards for many financial, telecommunications, transit, health care, access, and secure identification applications.

The name "smart card" is something of misnomer. While the plastic card was the initial smart card form factor, smart card technology is now available in wide variety of form factors, including plastic cards, key fobs, subscriber identification

---

[22] Eurosmart, Worldwide Smart Card Shipments, May 2010, www.eurosmart.com/index.php/publications/market-overview.html.

modules (SIMs) used in GSM mobile phones, watches, electronic passports, and USB-based tokens.

What started as an electronic device to store bank account information securely has evolved into a sophisticated computing device capable of supporting many different applications on a single card or token. These applications include bank cards, mobile phone SIMs, health-care cards, government and enterprise ID cards, benefits and social welfare cards, driver's licenses, physical and logical access cards, mass transit (ticketing) cards, and even cards that combine multiple applications on a single card.

How Smart Cards Communicate[23]

In general, smart cards do not display information or directly accept input from the user. For the user to access the information a smart card contains, the card needs an interface to communicate with a reader or terminal, such as a merchant POS terminal, a bank ATM, or a computer smart card reader. Data can be transferred either by physical contact, using electrical connections with the contact pads on the surface of the smart card, or without contact using radio frequency (RF) transmission.

The two methods of data transfer give rise to three types of smart cards: contact cards with a contact interface, contactless cards with a contactless RF interface, and dual-interface cards with both a contact interface and a contactless interface.

Contact Interface

A contact smart card's protocol interface is standardized in ISO/IEC 7816-3 while its physical connections are standardized in ISO/IEC 7816-2. Interfacing with the outside world requires the card to be inserted into a smart card reader or terminal in such a way that the smart card module makes a physical connection with the contact wiper pads within the reader device. Contact smart cards are used for many applications, including EMV credit/debit cards, health-care cards, national ID cards, and government and corporate employee ID cards that are used for accessing computers and networks.

---

[23] Smart Card Alliance, "What Makes a Smart Card Secure," October 2008.

Contactless Interface

A contactless smart card–based device includes an embedded secure microcontroller, internal memory, and a small antenna and communicates with a reader through an RF interface. The contactless interface provides users with the convenience of allowing the contactless device to be read at short distances with fast transfer of data.

There are two main differences between a contact and contactless smart card:

- There are no physical connections between the contactless card and the reader.
- A contactless card's power to drive the secure IC is derived from energy transferred from an RF field generated by the reader that induces an electrical current in the IC's antenna coil when it enters the reader's RF field (figure 1).

Contactless smart chip technology is available in a variety of forms: plastic cards, watches, key fobs, documents, and other handheld devices such as mobile phones. Contactless technology is used for applications such as mass transit tickets, physical access control, and debit and credit payment cards. Contactless mobile payment applications[24] are also now being implemented using Near Field Communication (NFC) technology, which is compatible with ISO/IEC 14443, the primary contactless smart card standard.

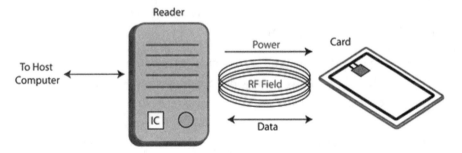

Figure 1. Contactless Smart Card in RF Field.

---

[24] Contactless mobile payment is also called proximity mobile payment.

Dual Interface

The dual-interface smart card has both a contact interface and a contactless interface. Physically, the card looks like a contact card, but the chip module has two additional contact points for the antenna coil. The chip can use either ISO/IEC 7816 or ISO/IEC 14443 protocols to communicate with a reader. Figure 2 shows an illustration of a dual-interface card.

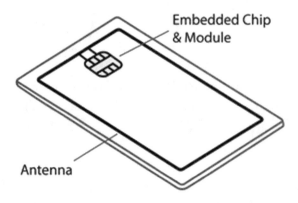

Figure 2. Dual-Interface Smart Card.

A dual-interface card may be required, for example, for a transit card, which requires the contactless mode for fast transaction times and throughput at turnstiles and the contact mode to allow funds to be reloaded at an ATM or merchant POS terminal.

Smart Cards and Payments

Both contact and contactless smart cards are used for many payment and payment-related applications worldwide. Smart card–based payment applications may be categorized across two dimensions:

- The configuration of the payment platform used to deliver payment functionality as either an open-loop payment system or closed-loop payment system.
- The storage location for the value that is available to the cardholder, either held as value in the memory of the card or held in an account in a back office.

The matrix in figure 3 provides an overview of the relationships between these two dimensions and provides examples for each category.

Payment Applications	Closed-Loop Payment System	Open-Loop Payment System
Card-Based Stored Value	• Traditional transit fare payment cards • SmartMeter parking card	• Visa Cash • Mondex
Back Office Account–Based	• Merchant-stored value cards • Gift cards • Electronic toll collection	• Bank-issued EMV credit and debit cards • Contactless bank cards

Figure 3. Payment Application Dimensions.

This chapter focuses on the use of smart cards for bank card payments.

Bank Card Payments

Bank cards are defined as any card issued by a bank that can access a consumer's financial resources, for example, bank cards, credit cards, debit cards, ATM cards, and prepaid cards. Bank cards, bank card message formats, and bank card processing requirements are defined by a variety of ISO/IEC standards[25] and specifications developed by the payments industry and payment brands.[26]

Bank Card Technology and Processing

Bank cards currently use two technologies to store account information and allow merchant POS terminals to read the information electronically: magnetic stripe technology and smart card technology.

Up until the late 1990s, magnetic stripe technology was used worldwide for

---

[25] Key standards include ISO/IEC 7810, ISO/IEC 7811, ISO/IEC 7812, ISO/IEC 7813, ISO/IEC 7816, ISO/IEC 8583, and ISO/IEC 14443.

[26] Industry specifications include EMV 4.2 and specifications from American Express, Discover, JCB, MasterCard, and Visa, which define the payment application and the security requirements for branded bank cards.

bank cards. The traditional magnetic stripe credit card payment transaction flow for an open-loop payment network (such as MasterCard or Visa) includes the following steps (shown in figure 4):

1. The merchant's POS system sends a transaction authorization request (including the cardholder account number, transaction amount, card verification code [CVC]/card verification value [CVV] for physical merchants) to the merchant acquirer/processor, who then sends it through the payment brands' financial networks to the card issuer.
2. The issuer performs the necessary security checks, authorizes or denies the transaction, and returns an authorization response to the merchant acquirer/processor, who passes it to the merchant.
3. Authorized transactions are captured (cleared) from the merchant every day, and a settlement message is sent over the financial networks to transfer funds to the merchant account.[27]

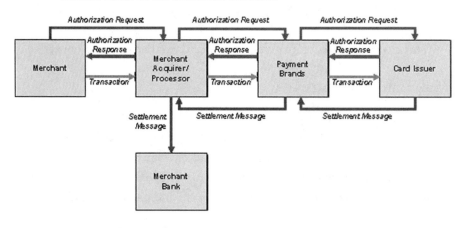

Figure 4. Credit Card Payment Transaction Flow.

Magnetic stripe card transactions rely on static account numbers. Because this data is static, the information can be easily stolen and reused to create a duplicate magnetic stripe card. This practice is known as skimming. Within the financial system, fraud checks are performed in the back-end systems to manage the risk of counterfeit or stolen cards being used.

---

[27] See additional discussion in Section 3.3.

Bank Card Payment with Smart Cards

Smart card technology introduced three significant factors to a payment card beyond what was provided by magnetic stripe card technology:

- The first is greater storage capacity for information. In comparison to the magnetic stripe, which holds 210 bits in track one and 75 bits in track two, the current smart card chips used in the payments industry have 2 kilobytes to 64 kilobytes, with chips available that have even greater storage capacity.
- The second factor is the ability to reliably write information back to the chip on the payment card at the time of the transaction.
- The third factor is the security provided by the microprocessor embedded in the chip along with the ability to load applications, not just data onto the chip.

Europay MasterCard Visa (EMV) Specifications

Increasing counterfeit card fraud led the financial industry to move to smart card technology for bank cards. Developed by Europay, MasterCard, and Visa (EMV), the EMV specification, first available in 1996, defines the global interoperable standard for smart bank cards. Since the initial release, JCB, Discover, and American Express have all joined in to support the EMV standards. As of the end of 2009, more than 944 million EMV payment cards were in use worldwide. Payment brand mandates and/or liability shifts have driven or are driving Europe, Asia, Africa, Latin America, and Canada to EMV. The United States is the only country with no current plans for EMV. Within the United States, however, contactless credit and debit cards are now being issued that include some EMV security features.

EMV Security

At the heart of EMV is the underlying security framework that provides fraud protection for both offline and online transactions. First, EMV leverages the security found in smart cards and requires symmetric authentication keys to gain access to the smart card's memory. This helps protect card stock in transit to issuers and in warehouse inventory, an important deterrent against the creation of authentic-looking counterfeit cards. Second is the EMV application logical security using special purpose symmetric access keys for personalization, post-issuance updates, and card and transaction authentication purposes. These keys help prevent unauthorized personalization of cards, secure transmission of card updates once they are in the cardholders' hands by encrypting all data that is to be sent to a card, authenticate a card and authorization request in an online transaction, and authenticate the issuer to the card.

Finally, asymmetric keys and certificates are incorporated to facilitate card authentication in offline transaction environments. Before an issuer can begin issuing EMV cards, an issuer's public key certificate must be obtained from the payment brands' certificate authority (CA). The issuer's public key certificate is loaded on each card that is issued. At the time of the transaction, the terminal authenticates the card's certificate by validating the issuer's public key certificate using the corresponding CA public key that is loaded onto the terminals by the payment brands. This process enables card authentication without online connectivity.

Issuers are provided three certificate implementation options: Static Data Authentication, Dynamic Data Authentication, and Combined Data Authentication. Each offers a different level of security to protect against card cloning, card skimming, and card data manipulation based on how the certificate is generated.

EMV Transaction Flow

With magnetic stripe cards, all risk management is performed during the transaction authorization process by a central system. The terminal simply serves the purpose of capturing the track one or two data and passing it through to the central server. With EMV, components of the risk assessment are pushed out to the terminal and the card to facilitate greater risk management for offline transactions. The issuer loads a set of risk management parameters into the EMV application on the chip. The terminal responds by performing each of the functions indicated by those risk parameters. The risk parameters range from the cardholder verification method (for example, requirement for a signature or PIN) to the form of cryptogram that is used for the card and terminal to perform an authentication routine. Other risk parameters address what the terminal should do under different authorization failure conditions or how a card can be used.

When the EMV card is inserted into the terminal, the terminal finds the EMV application and reads the EMV tags to get directions for handling the transaction. Both the terminal and the card perform an assessment to determine if the card should be declined, if the transaction should go online, or if it can be accepted as an offline transaction. If it is determined that the transaction requires an online authorization, a cryptogram is sent to the host system for final card and authorization validation. In response, the host calculates a response cryptogram and sends it back to the terminal to validate the issuer.

Contactless Credit/Debit Payment in the United States

Since mid-2005, leading financial issuers have placed tens of millions of contactless credit and debit cards and devices into the hands of consumers worldwide. Merchant acceptance has also increased dramatically over the past three years. Over 230,000 merchant locations[28] worldwide now accept contactless payments.

In a contactless payment transaction, the consumer holds the contactless card or device in close proximity (less than two to four inches) to the merchant POS terminal. The payment account information is communicated wirelessly via RF. Contactless payments in the United States are currently supported by multiple card issuers. American Express, Discover Network, MasterCard, and Visa all offer contactless payment products. These products rely on ISO/IEC 14443–based technology, ensuring payment solution compatibility regardless of brand or payment device when used with contactless readers that the payment brands have approved.

The initial introduction of contactless financial payment devices focused on markets that had lower-value transactions (less than $25), where consumers used cash for payment, and where transaction speed and customer convenience were critical. Contactless payments made quick progress in many merchant segments, including quick-service restaurants, convenience stores, pharmacies, theaters, and sports venues. Contactless payments have expanded beyond these initial merchant segments, however, moving into other traditional retail segments (for example, Best Buy and Office Depot) and opening up credit card acceptance in new merchant categories (for example, taxis, vending machines, and transit fare payment).

---

[28] MasterCard, www.paypass.com/performance_insights.html.

United States Contactless Payment Implementation Approach

In the United States, the payment brands implemented contactless payment transactions to leverage the existing magnetic stripe payments infrastructure. This approach facilitated straightforward contactless payment implementations by issuers, merchants, and payment processors and faster consumer adoption and merchant acceptance.

The same flow and process that is used for the traditional magnetic stripe credit card payment transaction (figure 5) applies to contactless financial payment transactions in the United States, with the following exceptions:

- Cardholder payment information is transferred to the POS system wirelessly using RF technology.
- At the card level, each contactless card can have its own unique built-in secret key that is used to generate a unique card verification value or a cryptogram that exclusively identifies each transaction.
- At the system level, payment networks have the ability to differentiate contactless and magnetic stripe transactions and automatically detect and reject any attempt to use the same transaction information more than once.
- Many contactless payment cards and devices do not transmit the name of the cardholder, limiting the amount of information that is communicated during the transaction.
- Some contactless payment cards and devices do not include the cardholder's account number, but use an alternate number that is associated with a payment account by the issuer's back-end processing system and cannot be used in other payment transactions (for example, with a magnetic stripe card or on the Internet).

Contactless Benefits

Table 1 summarizes the benefits of contactless to the key payment process participants

Payment Participant	Process	Benefit
Consumers[1]		Speed Convenience Coolness of new form factors Easy-to-use cash replacement Enhanced security and authentication
Merchants		Faster transactions[2] Customer convenience Increased customer spending[3] Reduced cash handling Improved operational efficiencies Reduced terminal maintenance Competitive differentiation Readiness for NFC proximity mobile payments Enhanced security and authentication
Issuers		Increased number of transactions "Top of wallet" status Increased spending per cardholder Improved customer retention Competitive differentiation (for example, form factors) Enhanced security and authentication

NFC Proximity Mobile Payments

The ability to pay for transit fares, groceries, and other products by simply waving a mobile phone near a POS device represents a new payment frontier. Such payments, called proximity mobile payments, are defined as payments to a merchant that are initiated from a mobile phone that uses NFC technology and is held close to the merchant's POS equipment.

NFC technology is a standards-based wireless communication technology that allows data to be exchanged between devices that are a few centimeters apart. NFC-enabled mobile phones incorporate smart chips (called secure elements) that allow the phones to securely store the payment application and consumer account information and use the information as a virtual payment card. NFC payment transactions between a mobile phone and a POS terminal use the standard ISO/IEC 14443 communication protocols currently used by contactless credit and debit cards.

Using NFC technology as the basis for proximity mobile payments leverages the infrastructure currently deployed to support contactless credit and debit card payments. Implementations around the world have produced consumer feedback that proximity mobile payment is easy and convenient.[29]

NFC will soon be available as standard functionality in many mobile phones and will allow consumers to perform safe contactless transactions, access digital content, and connect electronic devices simply. An NFC chip in a mobile device can act as a card, a reader, or both, enabling consumer devices to share information and make secure payments quickly.

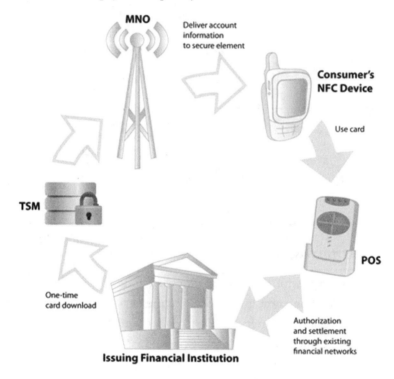

Figure 5. Proximity Mobile Payments Model.

For virtual payment cards to function on an NFC-enabled phone, a variety of entities must work together. Figure 5 illustrates the NFC proximity mobile payments model that is expected to be implemented. This model posits collaboration among financial institutions, the mobile network operator (MNO), and other stakeholders in the mobile payments ecosystem, including (potentially) a

---

[29] "Phones as Credit Cards? Americans Must Wait," *New York Times*, January 25, 2009.

trusted third party who manages the deployment of mobile applications (trusted service manager [TSM]).

Financial institutions prepare the account data and send the payment account information to a TSM. The TSM delivers the consumer's payment account information over the air (OTA) through the mobile network to the secure element in the mobile phone. Once the payment account is in the phone, the consumer can use the phone as a virtual payment card at merchants who accept contactless credit and debit payments. Payments are processed over the current financial networks.

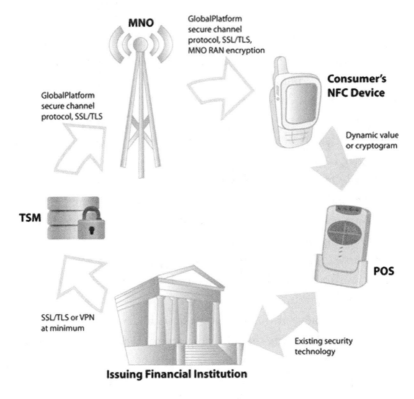

Figure 6. Security Mechanisms Used for Proximity Mobile Payments

Figure 6 illustrates the security mechanisms that protect the processes used in this model. Payment information personalization and lifecycle management from the issuer to the TSM are secured by standard Internet technologies, such as Secure Sockets Layer (SSL) or virtual private networks (VPNs). GlobalPlatform's secure channel protocol provides for the communication and storage of sensitive account data between the TSM and the secure element in the mobile device.

Account data is further kept secure from OTA sniffing by encryption provided by the MNO. When the consumer uses the NFC device for payment, the transaction is protected using the same security mechanisms in place for contactless credit and debit cards.

Conclusions

The smart card has a thirty-year history in enabling ease of use for electronic transactions and adding security to payments involving cards and other form factors. In addition to its retail payments roots, the technology has been adopted by the mobile industry and transportation industry, for government passports, national ID programs, and corporate identity and security systems, and, most recently, for an entire new generation of intelligent devices that enable secure machine-to-machine communications.

Of the 4.5 billion microprocessor smart cards shipped in 2009, only about one out of six is used for financial payments, so the recent ups and downs of the financial markets has had little effect on overall demand overall. Forecasters predict another 10 percent growth in 2010. The current market is a fraction of total worldwide market potential with financial markets in many parts of the world still having huge growth potential. Other than Europe and parts of Asia and Latin America that have already fully migrated to smart cards, chip migration is just starting in large regions around the world, like the United States, China, and Africa. The United States payment card market alone, with around 700 million non-smart cards in circulation, is about equal in size to the shipment of financial smart cards in 2009.

The core technology attributes that make smart cards so universal for all of these diverse applications are the fully programmable microprocessor chip, the advanced anti-tampering and anti-cloning designs of the chip design, the capability to encrypt and store data in a readable/writable way, and the small footprint and form factor versatility that allow smart card chips to fit into a thin plastic card, a mobile phone, a passport booklet, or even a watch. Having the ability to communicate through a contact surface module inside a reader or use RF over controlled distances makes smart cards adaptable to the varied and changing conditions of the payments industry, from complex, authenticated, PIN-based, offline EMV (chip and PIN) credit card purchases to subsecond read/write fare transactions on a bus or subway.

The ability to adapt smart card technology to changing market conditions and varied payments infrastructures may be best highlighted by the different approaches taken by countries who have standardized payments security around the EMV standard versus countries like the United States, Japan, and South Korea who have adopted contactless smart card payments using alternative security protocols. Despite the differences outlined in this chapter, the approaches have common elements so there is a path to EMV compatibility for EMV and contactless payments.

This chapter concludes with a brief introduction to NFC technology for mobile phones. NFC is a new mobile technology that leverages the ability for the NFC-enabled phone to emit a short-range RF communication compatible to current contactless payment cards. This enables NFC proximity mobile payment. NFC phones are programmed securely OTA via the mobile carrier's network under agreements with an issuing bank and TSM. The process safely manages cardholder data inside the mobile device's Universal Integrated Circuit Card (UICC) or Universal Subscriber Identity Module (USIM) chip and enables the NFC phone to deliver payment account data to the existing contactless merchant POS devices that accept contactless payment cards. NFC proximity mobile payments bring a new dimension to the smart card payments market because it combines the rich user interface of a keyboard and display with the always-connected mobile network. This enables consumers to use Web browsing to search for merchants, receive promotion messages or coupons right on their phone, and transact a purchase in a store in real time with the same security that contactless payment cards offer.

In the new always-connected, networked world, smart card technology is fueling innovative applications, enabling secure transactions, and providing the security that consumers need to protect private information.

CHAPTER TEN

GETTING CAUGHT IN THE RIPTIDE: THE EVOLUTION OF ONLINE IDENTITY THEFT

LAURA MATHER, PH.D., SILVER TAIL SYSTEMS

ONLINE identity theft is one of the main ways fraud is perpetrated at financial institutions. The 2009 Javelin Identity Fraud Survey Report showed that, in 2008, 9.9 million adults (an increase of 22 percent year over year) in the United States were victims of identity fraud and the annual fraud amount was $48 billion (an increase of 7 percent year over year).

Identity theft is not a new crime, but the popularity of the Internet has made it extremely easy to both steal and use online identities. By understanding how online identity theft has changed since its inception, financial institutions can better understand the criminals' motivations and determine effective techniques for combating them.

The definition of online identity theft is simple, the use of credentials or identifying information by a third party. In most cases, the stolen identity is used to transfer money out of a bank account, but there are other ways criminals can benefit from obtaining identity-related information from their victims. For example, the criminals can apply for credit or loans in the name of the victim. Or the criminal could perpetrate a pump-and-dump scam. In this case, the criminal opens a brokerage account, say at Brokerage C, and buys shares of a penny stock. Next, the criminal signs into the victim's brokerage account, say at Brokerage V, and uses the victim's money to buy additional shares of the penny stock. Because the victim's money is used to buy the penny stock, this raises the price of the penny stock. At which point, the criminal goes back to his account at Brokerage C and sells the shares for a hefty profit.

There are many reasons why online identity theft is increasing. The first is obvious. Given that online identity theft is an industry worth $48 billion per year, it is clearly an exceedingly profitable enterprise. The other reason for the continued increase in this type of crime is that it is extremely unlikely that the criminal will be caught. The inventors of the Internet were brilliant in creating an infrastructure that is extremely flexible and scalable. But many of the mechanisms that make the Internet powerful also make it easy for the criminals to perpetrate their crimes almost completely anonymously. For example, when sending an e-mail, the sender can specify any from address, even if the sender does not have access to the domain of that address. So, if a criminal wants to send an e-mail and pretend the sender is from bankABC.com, it is very easy to do so. Also, when the criminal interacts with Web sites, it is very easy for the criminal to use proxies (machines that allow Web traffic to pass through them) to hide the actual location of the criminal. This makes it excessively difficult for banks and law enforcement to track down the perpetrator during the investigation of the crime.

Not only does technology make it difficult to find the criminals, but prosecuting them can be close to impossible. When the criminal is sitting in Europe, the machine used to perpetrate the crime is in Asia, and the victim is in the United States, it can be very challenging to determine which laws and jurisdictions apply to the crime. While cooperation between international law enforcement has improved in recent years, there are still many challenges to be overcome.

Given that online identity theft continues to be profitable for the criminals, it's important to understand its origins and how it has evolved. This chapter will talk about three aspects of online identity theft:

- We'll cover the victim and how criminals are now targeting commercial enterprises much more frequently than they have in the past.
- We'll talk about the mechanisms for stealing identities, including phishing and malware.
- We'll discuss the advancement of the criminal infrastructure.

Changes in Identity Theft Targets

There have been several changes in the targets of online identity theft. In this section, we will outline some of those changes.

Two types of shifts in identity theft targets were originally identified around 2007. This was the move from phishing to either spear phishing or whaling. In phishing, the criminals usually don't know the demographics of their potential victims. They will send e-mails to lists of e-mail addresses without knowing if those e-mail addresses correspond to a customer of the financial institution. This technique has one main disadvantage. Because the probability that the e-mail recipient will be a customer of the targeted financial institution is low, a very large number of e-mails need to be sent to guarantee enough stolen credentials. When large numbers of e-mails are sent, it is more likely spam filters will determine that the e-mail is fraudulent and block it. Spear phishing and whaling are two ways to avoid the problem of needing to send large numbers of e-mails.

In spear phishing, the phisher sends e-mails to people who are very likely to be customers of a particular financial institution. The best example of this is credit unions that support a particular organization. For example, if a university has a credit union, sending phishing e-mail to e-mail addresses on that university's domain has a higher likelihood of reaching someone who is a customer of that credit union than sending e-mails to random e-mail addresses. Similarly, some companies have credit unions specifically catering to that company's employees.

In whaling, the phishers send much more targeted e-mails to very high-profile individuals. In this case, the phisher will research a particular company. It is often possible to determine which bank the company uses as well as the names and e-mail addresses of the company's executives. Using this information, the phisher will craft very sophisticated e-mail that is sent only to the company's executives in hopes of obtaining credentials for the company's bank account.

Another shift that has been seen recently is that from targeting consumers to targeting small and medium businesses. Traditionally, online identity theft has targeted more consumers than businesses. In the typical case, the criminal would obtain the credentials of the victim and use those credentials to transfer money out of the victim's personal savings or checking account. But there has been a shift in the past twelve months that shows the criminals targeting small and medium businesses for online identity theft instead of individual consumers.

While it is difficult to determine exactly why there has been a shift from consumers to businesses, one possibility has to do with Regulation E. Regulation E "limits a consumer's liability for unauthorized electronic funds transfers to $50." This means banks must reimburse consumers for any money above $50 taken from the consumer's account by an unauthorized party.

Why would Regulation E impact who the criminals target for identity theft? To answer this question, you have to look at the incident from the financial institution's point of view. Let's consider an oversimplified scenario. Assume you are the vice president of risk management for Bank ABC . Your bonuses are predicated by the amount of money the bank loses to online identity theft. You have two kinds of accounts you are protecting: consumer accounts and commercial accounts. Every time money is stolen from a consumer account, the bank must reimburse the consumer for everything except $50. Many banks reimburse the entire amount. This is a loss to the bank. In contrast, when money is stolen from a commercial account, the bank is not required to reimburse the company for the money, though some banks will reimburse businesses for this, resulting in no loss to the bank.

As vice president of risk management, you have limited resources to deploy tools and other resources to detect and prevent money from being stolen from accounts. Where would you prioritize your resources: protecting consumer accounts or protecting commercial accounts? Many of the larger financial institutions deploy similar risk detection platforms for both their consumer and commercial businesses, but the smaller financial institutions often may have to choose to protect one type of account more than another. As we'll discuss later, the criminals are continually optimizing their processes. If it is easier for criminals to steal money from commercial bank accounts, it is likely that commercial accounts will be targeted.

The Progression of Credential Theft Mechanisms

Another component of identity theft that has changed recently is the mechanism by which the criminals steal online identities. The original form of stealing identities online was phishing, the process of stealing personal information by masquerading as a trusted brand through electronic communication. Most phishing is communicated through e-mail, but there have been cases of phishing through instant message services, cell phone text messages, and even landline phone calls. The first documented case of phishing was in 1987, but this was to steal passwords to e-mail accounts for sending spam. Phishing against financial institutions did not become prevalent until 2003. The typical timeline for phishing looks something like this:

- Phisher creates Web site that resembles Bank ABC's Web site.
- Phisher sends e-mail pretending to be Bank ABC and telling the victim to go to fake Web site.
- Victim receives e-mail and enters credentials on fake banking Web site.
- Criminal uses credentials on real Bank ABC Web site to transfer money out of the victim's account.

Several countermeasures have been implemented to protect against this kind of attack. The countermeasures correspond to the different components of the phishing attack. Because the phisher is sending e-mail, in most cases, to initiate the phishing attacks, financial institutions will work with Internet service providers (ISPs) to attempt to block the potential victim from receiving the phishing e-mails. This is challenging because there are many ways the phisher can change the e-mail to get around spam filters to ensure that the e-mail is delivered.

Next, because the victim enters his credentials on the fake Web site, the financial institutions will find these Web sites and work with ISPs and Web hosting companies to get them shut down. This is proving to be effective. A study done by the Anti-Phishing Working Group showed that, for the first half of 2009, the average uptime for phishing Web sites was thirty-nine hours, with a median of thirteen hours and fifteen minutes. This was down significantly from an average of fifty-two hours and median of fourteen hours and forty-three minutes in the second half of 2008.

Finally, because the criminal will be using the victim's credentials on the financial institution's Web site, the financial institution will implement security mechanisms to detect when a third party is using the victim's credentials. Example detection mechanisms include IP geolocation and device identification. IP geolocation verifies the IP address being used by the person currently signed in to the account is similar to the geolocation of the IP address originally used on the account. Device identification verifies the computer currently accessing the account is the same as the computer that originally accessed the account. Both of these can be effective ways of detecting phishing because the phishers would be accessing the bank account from a different location and computer than the victim.

As with most criminal exploits, countermeasures put in place to protect against a specific attack vector often result in the criminals escalating their attacks to get around the countermeasures. The crime of identity theft is no exception. The response to protection mechanisms financial institutions were deploying against phishing led to the rise in the use of malware for identity theft.

Because financial institutions were able to get phishing Web sites shut down faster, the criminals had to find other ways to steal credentials. One way to do this is through malware, software installed on a computer without the computer owner's permission. Malware comes in many forms, but, in this case, the most relevant type of malware is keystroke loggers. Keystroke loggers record all keystrokes performed on a computer and send that information back to the criminal. The criminal can parse this information to identify user IDs and passwords for online accounts as well as other personal information like name, address, phone number, credit card numbers, and so forth.

When financial institutions moved to using geolocation and device identification to detect the use of accounts by unauthorized third parties, the identity thieves had to find a way to get around these detection techniques. This resulted in several uses of malware.

The first use of malware to evade geolocation and device identification was for proxy IP addresses. Criminals installed malware on consumer machines that would allow them to route Internet traffic through the infected computer. Now when a phisher had credentials from an individual in Sarasota, Florida, and wanted to access that victim's bank account, he could find an infected computer near Sarasota and route his Internet session through that computer. That way, when the bank performed a geolocation lookup on that IP address, it would see that the geolocation was similar to that of the victim, so the session looked less suspicious.

Circumventing device identification is a bit trickier, but the criminals are tenacious. One method they've found to fool device identification systems is Man-in-the-Browser (MitB) attacks. Figure 1 shows a MitB attack. Malware infections can happen in many ways, but figure 1 shows an e-mail received by the victim that includes a link to a Web site that downloads malware onto the victim's computer. The first step in figure 1 shows the e-mail being sent to the victim. The e-mail's purpose is to lure the victim to an infected Web site. By clicking the link in the e-mail, the victim is taken to the infected Web site (step two). In the third step, the infected Web site installs its malware onto the victim's computer. In the MitB case, the malware is often in the form of a browser plugin. MitB malware is especially devious in that it stays dormant until the victim visits his bank or other targeted Web site. In the fourth step, when the victim logs in to the targeted Web site, the malware comes alive and creates a second session (invisible to the victim). So, while the victim is doing his normal activity on the Web site, the malware is performing its nefarious activity in the background using the computer, IP address, and session of the victim.

Man in the Browser Attack

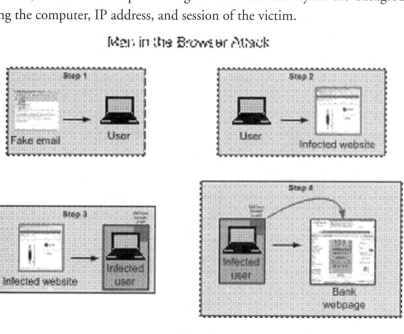

Figure 1

There are at least two other kinds of MitB attacks:

- One captures the victim's information as he types it into the browser and sends it back to the criminal. This MitB attack then becomes a Man-in-the-Middle attack because the criminal will use the victim's credentials, but won't be using the victim's machine. This can be used to circumvent second factor authentication because the second factor credentials can be sent to the criminal in real time for the criminal to use immediately.
- In the second, the malware will wait for the victim to perform a

high-value transaction (for example, transferring money out of their account) on the legitimate Web site. When the victim performs this transaction, the malware modifies the transaction so it is beneficial to the criminal. For example, the malware might modify a transaction that is supposed to transfer money to the victim's brokerage account and instead transfer a larger amount of money to the criminal's bank account. This type of MitB attack is rare because it requires the victim to perform the exact transaction the criminal wants to perform, so it has a lower conversion rate for the criminal. Many forms of malware, including Zeus and Clampi, perpetrate MitB attacks.

The countermeasures to these malware attacks can be challenging. The criminals have gotten very good at changing the malware so each instance has a different signature. This means that antivirus software can have a difficult time detecting the malware because most antivirus algorithms are based on looking for signatures. Some antivirus companies are moving toward a more behavior-based approach. In this case, the software monitors all of the processes on a computer and looks for processes that are behaving in ways that are unexpected.

The other countermeasure to attacks like MitB is to monitor Web site traffic and look at the behavior of users on the Web site. A MitB Web site session will look very different from a normal user session. By monitoring all sessions, it is possible to identify those that are MitB.

The Underground Economy

A Federal Trade Commission survey estimates that 3.25 million American adults had their personal data used in online identity theft in 2003. This is less than one-third of the number of people impacted by online identity theft in 2008. What has changed?

When online identity theft was first starting around 2003, twentysomethings in Eastern Europe mostly perpetrated it. At that time, phishing e-mails had many spelling and grammar errors. Phishing sites were hosted on domains that were registered specifically for the purpose of phishing. In general, it was a sloppy enterprise.

Starting in 2007, things changed. It became very obvious to those who fight phishing that the phishers had evolved. No longer were the e-mails sloppy. No longer was it fairly easy to get phishing Web sites shut down. Investigation showed that the phishing community had organized. Forensics on e-mails, Web sites, and the use of stolen credentials showed there were subgroups within the phishing underground economy. There were individual groups for acquiring the domains to use to host the phishing Web sites, writing the e-mails, sending the e-mails, validating the credentials received on the Web site, and then using the credentials to steal the money. All of these groups worked very well together. And all of these groups were very savvy in their particular area of expertise.

Phishing is a business. In the 2007 time frame, the phishers became very good at their business. They seemed to be optimizing for conversion rates and returns, just like a legitimate business. But, of course, the phishers didn't have the encumbrance of having to subscribe to ethics or moral codes.

With the evolution of malware, we continue to see a sophisticated underground economy. There are groups that write the malware, groups that sell malware distributions (infected computers), and groups that sell compromised credentials.

The technological expertise and overall coordination of these online criminals is extremely scary.

Going Forward

Given the sophistication and synchronization of the attacks against financial services Web sites, where do we go from here? First, it seems inevitable that the current detection mechanisms, things like IP geolocation and device identification, are not going to be enough to combat the persistent onslaught of fraud. It is likely that risk management teams at financial institutions are going to have to move in the same direction as antivirus vendors, looking for behavior anomalies instead of attack signatures.

In addition, it will be increasingly important to anticipate the responses to various fraud prevention measures. If a particular fraud prevention measure is put in place and the criminals move to an even more harmful attack vector, that could be detrimental for the entire financial industry. Responding to identity theft is critical, but it is also extremely important to respond in a measured way such that the consequences aren't worse than the original situation.

Finally, because the criminals are now working together, it is imperative that financial institutions continue to work together. By identifying new threats and sharing data that can be used to recognize a specific attack, financial institutions can make each attack less profitable for the criminals, thereby reducing the incentive for committing the fraud.

Online identity theft has evolved in many ways. Understanding this evolution can help us anticipate where it is going and prepare us for the continued fight against this destructive force.

CHAPTER ELEVEN

BENEFITS OF NEUTRAL SECURE
ELEMENT FOR MOBILITY

SIVA NARENDRA, TYFONE

TO prevent fraudulent transactions while allowing legitimate ones involves trade-offs between cost, convenience, and security. These trade-offs must be dynamic because technology and threat models continuously evolve.

Online electronic commerce has been growing steadily over the past decade. This creates the potential for more and increasingly sophisticated fraud because the potential return, albeit illegal, is ever increasing. It is evident that the convenience and therefore the growth of online electronic commerce has also led to a wide range of remote fraud methods, ranging from simple phishing Web sites to more sophisticated and organized domain hijacking.

While online electronic commerce by definition is applicable for remote transactions, mobile commerce, which is perceived as an evolution of online commerce, is applicable for both online transactions and offline brick-and-mortar transactions.

This is because mobile devices are with consumers most of the time, enabling offline use cases. The mobile devices are almost always connected to the network, enabling online uses as well as possible hybrid use cases. Note that, for the definitive coverage of commerce use cases, you should be able to perform online use cases when you don't have or don't want to use your mobile device, and you should be able to do offline use cases even if the mobile device is not connected to the network.

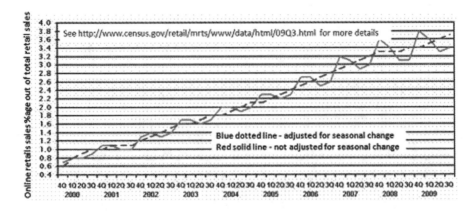

While online electronic commerce has been growing steadily since 2000, it still represents only about 4 percent of retail sales in the United States, as reported by the United States Census Bureau in November 2009. As mentioned above, mobile devices enable both online and offline use cases. With potentially 100 percent of the retail market being addressable by such devices, the chances of attracting fraud as mobile commerce evolves are rather significant.

Secure Element

The ability to prevent fraud while allowing legitimate access strongly relies on the factors of authentication used. Factors of authentication can be divided into three types: what you know (such as PIN), what you have (such as a SIM card), or who you are (such as your fingerprint). The more factors of authentication used, the greater the likelihood of preventing fraud. This, of course, results in potential inconvenience and increased cost, thus the need for trade-offs between the cost, convenience, and security as described earlier.

The goals of fraud prevention are not just about appropriate methods of authentication, but also about protecting the identity of the consumer and the information that is being exchanged after authentication. This is often accomplished by encoding and encrypting the information with the help of appropriate algorithms, associated keys, key management, and security engineering.

An underlying assumption of these goals is that the engineering methods have the ability to securely store some key pieces of information so a consumer's fingerprint can be verified or information be encrypted.

In online-only uses, as supported by electronic commerce, it is reasonable to assume that this secure lockbox is available only in the back-end server infrastructure. By virtue of the online connection between the server and the consumer's client device, security engineering methods can be implemented with the lockbox available remotely. Mobile commerce requires online and offline access, so the lockbox must also be available locally in the client device. Without this, mobile commerce will not completely address consumer expectations.

Secure local information storage is accomplished through SIM card chips or smart card chips. These are called secure elements. SIM cards are used by the telecommunication industry; Smart cards are used by other identity management sectors, including payment, government, and corporate.

These secure elements, especially the smart card chips and their associated software framework, are often designed specifically to manage various threat models as defined and tested under the Common Criteria for Information Technology Security Evaluation (www.commoncriteriaportal.org).

Smart card chips come with dual interfaces: one is a contact interface that follows ISO7816 standards and the other is a contactless RFID interface that follows ISO14443 standards.

Using such a secure element in a manner compatible with mobile devices will seamlessly enable online and offline use cases. Near Field Communication or NFC technology, attempts to do this natively in a mobile device. Unfortunately, NFC hasn't caught on for multiple reasons, which we cover in the next section while providing a potential long-term solution.

Neutrality

Part of the reason why NFC for ubiquitous mobile commerce has not been successful is that the secure element used in the majority of NFC implementations was the SIM card. SIM cards were fundamentally meant for the identification of mobile subscribers for telecom services. The telecom service provider takes on fraud liability associated with owning that secure element and the information it contains. Mobile telecom service providers cannot take liability for all the commerce identities that might be stored in a SIM card, unless, of course, transaction fees, already a contentious matter, are shared with the mobile telecom service provider as an insurance policy against fraud. The issue of secure element ownership and its associated fraud liability has limited the growth of NFC.

Additionally, from a consumer's perspective, given that he will have one mobile service provider relationship, but multiple payment and other identities, it is important to be able to choose each provider independently. A SIM-centric solution will not accomplish the consumer independence necessary in the long run for wide-scale adoption, unless mandated by a regulatory body. The importance of this neutrality and independence is best explained by an example from the early history of electronic commerce.

In the early 1980s, when electronic commerce was in its infancy, wired network operators believed that, by managing both the network and its commerce content, they could deliver additional value to consumers. An example of such an initiative was Viewtron, which essentially determined the nature of content delivered through their network service. While initially successful, this service ultimately limited consumer choice due to the coupled relationship between content and network, causing the business to fail. Services such as AOL that subsequently attempted to control content were also unsuccessful. In the 1990s, the consumer's freedom of choice prevailed through the invention of Web servers and Web browsers. This technology and the services it enables are inherently neutral, decoupling content providers from network operators, resulting in the growth of PC-driven electronic commerce.

Fast-forward to the twenty-first century. With the way NFC was initially defined when mobile commerce was in its infancy, we see this history repeating itself. This time, the mobile ecosystem would like to manage the network as well as the commerce content. Mobile devices, unlike PCs, are relevant for both online and offline commerce use cases, as discussed earlier. Offline commerce still dwarfs online commerce, and mobile-driven commerce is therefore relevant to a wider variety of ecosystem participants than PC-driven commerce. Given that NFC requires consumer identities to be stored in the mobile provider–owned secure element, such as a SIM card or UICC, which, by definition, is non-neutral, the wider variety of ecosystem participants have been unwilling to enable this potentially useful technology.

This conundrum can be solved if we set out to build a neutral technology that will bring to mobile commerce what Web technology brought to the online electronic commerce. The memory card slot ubiquitous in mobile devices is one possible way to provide the neutrality and independence a consumer needs. This also has the potential to resolve the problem of secure element ownership versus the fraud liability of identities stored in a single secure element.

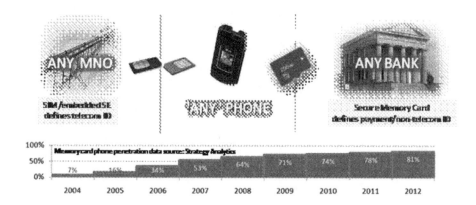

In the world of electronic commerce from the advent of non-neutral Viewtron to commercialization of web based neutral technology it took over a dozen years. It has been nearly a decade since standards for SIM based NFC was published for mobile commerce. Now with the advent of neutral secure element, in the decade of 2010, we can kick start mobile commerce!

CHAPTER TWELVE

THE ROLE OF THE ONLINE CHANNEL IN PAYMENTS FRAUD

CRAIG PRIESS, GUARDIAN ANALYTICS

CYBER criminals have it figured out. With lax security and fraud detection measures in place, the online customer account is now the preferred entry point for diverting millions and perhaps billions of dollars out of the bank balances of consumers and businesses. Payments channels and types play a key role in how cyber criminals extract these funds using a variety of sophisticated techniques.

John, for example, loved the simplicity of online banking, which he could use from home or work, making it easier than ever to keep his finances in order. Unfortunately, his son used the home computer to surf the Web and inadvertently visited a Web site that installed keylogging malware. The software sent John's online banking account user name and password to a cyber criminal, who accessed the account, obtained the account balance, and viewed scanned images of recent checks to see the sequence number, signature block, and MICR strip. From there, it was easy to forge counterfeit checks that easily passed traditional check fraud controls.

In a more sophisticated version of this fraud, a cyber criminal used an e-mail–based phishing scheme to steal personal information about a customer of a large credit union. He was able to call the credit union's customer service number and convince an agent to change the online account password and contact phone number. The thief then accessed the online account, downloaded check images, and learned more about the customer's account and online activities. He used the new information to open an account in the customer's name at a second bank and then arranged a wire transfer from the victimized account to the new account. Because the names on the accounts were the same and the thief could verify his identity with a phone number and even a signature, the wire transfer was authorized. The fraudster then withdrew the money from the new account using multiple branches in a state different than the victim's, eliminating detection until all the funds had been withdrawn.

Businesses are vulnerable, too. An elaborate scheme involving unwitting mules and multiple financial institutions recently hit a community bank based in the Midwest. Probably using keylogging malware, the perpetrator obtained the online account credentials of an authorized employee of a small nonprofit customer. After the fact, session logs revealed that the cyber criminal performed account reconnaissance the day before the theft, examining account balances and transaction history, and even modifying a pending ACH transaction. The next day, the fraudster executed an ACH batch file containing sixteen separate debit transfers (each of them under $9,000 to stay undetected) for a total withdrawal of $142,000. The transfers were sent to accounts at eight banks, all larger institutions, in states throughout the United States. The recipient accounts belonged to unwitting mules who thought they had been hired (over the Internet, of course) to do legitimate jobs. The mules were instructed to empty the funds from their accounts the day the money arrived, use Western Union to send the money to bogus fraudster identities in Texas and Florida, and keep 5 percent of the amount as a commission. In this case, a debit alert system and quick ACH reversals blocked twelve out of the sixteen transfers, but $36,000 was still unrecoverable.

The Online Channel and ACH

The sad reality is that, in making online banking easy, convenient, and feature-rich, which is a key to adoption, banks have also made it easy and convenient for cyber criminals to steal money and account information, which is used to actualize fraud outside the online channel. In addition to committing counterfeit check and wire transfer fraud, common fraud schemes include call center fraud in which the fraudster uses the stolen information simply to call the bank's call center and request a wire transfer or other account manipulation. Another is debit card fraud in which the criminal uses the online account to change the account address and request a new debit card, which is then used to empty the account.

But one of the fastest growing fraud schemes using stolen online account information is based on the ACH system. Criminal focus on ACH fraud is the result of the fundamental change in how the ACH system is being used. Originally designed solely for the transfer of funds between two known and trusted parties (for example, direct deposit to employees), the system has built-in security commensurate with its original uses. But ACH is being used today for one-off transactions by parties who may know nothing about each other. Retail and consumer online banking platforms make it easy for account holders (or fraudsters who have taken over accounts) to initiate ACH transactions. Armed with access to a compromised online banking account, a fraudster can easily start pulling money out of a victim's account by simply verifying a micro-deposit amount as part of a common ACH account-to-account setup process.

Exact fraud loss numbers are hard to come by. Unauthorized return rates offer some guidance and have held steady over the last couple years, but transaction volume has grown steadily with Internet-initiated entries experiencing double-digit growth rates. More than ever, to protect ACH, an institution must protect online banking, a good thing in today's world of increasing cyber crime.

Countering the Online Threat

Despite the seemingly unlimited number of schemes that cyber criminals can spin once they've stolen online bank account information, there is some good news. By adopting the following best practices, banks can prevent or detect many fraud attempts and dramatically reduce their losses while better protecting their customers.

- **Correlate online session activity with offline activity.** An online breach is often just the first step of a cross-channel scheme in which the funds are diverted using another channel. The online customer account has become a reconnaissance bonanza for cyber criminals.
- **Accurately assess the role of the online channel in fraud cases.** Banks often use the last offline step in a cross-channel scheme to categorize the type of fraud, thereby underestimating the size of the problem of the online channel and under-funding their investment in online anti-fraud measures.
- **Monitor online activity even after successful logins to reveal suspicious behavior.** Criminals rely on their online account reconnaissance

to go undetected. By recognizing in-session anomalous behavior as it occurs, it's possible to shut down fraudulent activity before a loss.

- **Beware of new retail bank accounts created online when large sums of money start moving.** Immediately begin tracking the activity of all related accounts.
- **When one account is compromised, immediately look for others.** Fraudsters work hard to exploit an institution's processes and controls and often use this knowledge across multiple attacks.
- **Regularly update fraud detection methods with the latest technologies.** Even with smart people and consistent processes in place, legacy fraud detection technologies can be blind to the latest fraudster techniques. Fraud prevention is an arms race. Plan on continual investment.

Predictive Modeling Detects What Other Technologies Can't

The biggest weakness of attacks starting with the online channel is that, no matter how careful the criminals are, their behavior won't follow the pattern established by the legitimate account holder. For most people and businesses, banking tends to be routine with regular patterns of deposits, withdrawals, and balance checking. Thanks to new technology, predictable behavior modeling can be used to detect the anomalies created by a cyber criminal's reconnaissance activities in real time following a successful breach.

These technologies go far beyond the use of simple machine signatures or rules. Instead, they use rich analytics to understand the individual usage patterns of every account holder. This is extremely important because any session anomaly must be compared to a single individual's typical activity, not to some aggregate abstract pattern applied to all or segments of customers. Today's dynamic, model-based analysis of individual account behavior is able to piece together events that, by themselves, may seem meaningless. But, stitched together, they reveal a clear pattern of suspicious behavior that just might be fraud.

The more the behavior pattern deviates from the customer's typical pattern, the higher the risk. The more information predictive modeling has to work with, the more powerful it is. When the assessment is based on correlating all available information, including machine information, network information, temporal information, and a user's non-transaction behavior, the bank's fraud team can obtain very granular risk scoring, allowing it to focus on the biggest and most obvious threats, detecting them earlier, and preventing or reversing them.

Cyber Criminals Stopped in Their Tracks

Many attacks on the online channel involve anomalous account behavior that can be analyzed to detect and stop them. Whether it's a fraudster using keylogging malware to obtain sufficient personal account information to create authentic-looking forged checks or a more sophisticated cyber criminal devising elaborate schemes to use the ACH system to send money to unwitting mules, the technology exists to thwart them.

Organizations like NACHA, the Electronic Payments Association, and the Financial Services Technology Consortium (FSTC) are working to provide the banking industry with as much information as possible to understand the online threat, and vendors are busy coming up with technology solutions that will make earlier fraud detection possible. While we will never prevent all fraud, the amount of online account session information available for analysis works both ways. It makes it easier for cyber criminals to steal credentials, but it also enables platforms with predictive modeling capabilities to get the insight they need to create ever more sophisticated models that power better real-time detection. With the right information and the right best practices, institutions can make a serious dent in preventing fraud that starts in the online channel.

CHAPTER THIRTEEN

COMBINING IMAGE TECHNOLOGY AND BEHAVIORAL ANALYTICS TO WIN THE WAR ON CHECK FRAUD

KEVIN ROPER, SCOTT WEST AND STEVEN SCHAEFFER, FIS

S ENIOR executives, board members, risk managers, and the insurance companies who write policies for financial institutions face a substantial shared risk from check fraud. It is imperative for financial executives to assess the risk and exposure and determine all the real and hidden costs they will assume if they are victimized by check fraud.

In 2008, 91 percent of institutions affected by attempted or actual payments fraud were victims of check fraud. Historically, financial institutions have been liable for these losses. While check volumes are declining at more than 4 percent per year on a nationwide basis, the National Check Fraud Center reports that checks remain a preferred target for criminals committing payments fraud. Organized check fraud gangs constantly try new technologies to beat the banking system and steal money from depositors. Organized check fraud gangs continue to introduce new schemes designed to beat the banking system and steal money from depositors.

What does this mean for financial institutions across the country? It means an increasing per check loss for every recorded incidence of check fraud. It also means that it is time for financial executives to combine the latest breakthroughs in image technology and behavioral analytics to reduce the financial exposure to their banks and shareholders and turn the tide on check fraud.

Preventing Check Frauds Before They Become Losses

Fortunately, there are highly sophisticated yet affordable fraud detection solutions such as ACH Positive Pay (with optional payee name verification), fraud detection filters, and teller alert systems to help identify and prevent check frauds before they become significant losses. Used in tandem, these applications combine to create a synergy that increases the value of the solution far beyond that of each individual component.

Each year, financial institutions unwittingly accept hundreds of millions of fraudulent checks for deposit. Fraudulent items are written against consumer, commercial, and even official bank accounts and presented for payment or deposit at the teller window. With billions of checks crossing their stations each year, tellers have little time to inspect and verify them all. Teller alert systems allow tellers to stop check frauds on the spot.

FIS's Teller Alert solution produces warnings within the bank's teller platform when fraudulent acts are detected at the point of first presentment. Teller Alert can pull information regarding the current transaction from both Positive Pay and the fraud filter systems. Positive Pay information, including the payee, can be displayed in a record-matching format for confirmation, or the system can produce an alert that the records do not match.

Fraud detection filters serve up information and graphs about the transaction's item amount and serial frequency, as well as searching special watch and alert tables for accounts with elevated suspicious activity. Some of the industry-leading fraud detection filter solutions offer up to twelve different filters for monitoring and alerting suspects within the check processing data stream.

More sophisticated offerings provide the ability to import ACH items into a fraud detection filter review scope so both converted items and high-risk ACH transactions can be monitored.

When run through a filter monitoring system, checks are scrutinized by their behavioral context within an account. Filters for check kiting, serial and amount variance, high dollar, and special watch can combine to identify, manage, and prevent suspicious and potentially costly fraudulent transactions from entering the payments system.

Fraud detection filters can provide a powerful and effective complement to new account screening products. Recently, a $50 billion-asset financial institution utilizing fraud filters reported savings on suspected items in the amount of $72 million (on deposited items for 2008).

Combining Behavioral Analytics and Image Technology

Many financial institutions run these systems separately or run them side-by-side with minimal information sharing. Financial institutions are now realizing the benefits of combining behavioral analytics and image technology to provide a comprehensive approach to check fraud prevention, including automated signature verification, check stock validation, serial variance tracking, amount variance tracking (deposit/check), and frequency tracking (deposit/check).

Industry-leading fraud detection suites combine the scores from multiple risk engines to identify and prioritize the greatest fraud risks:

- Combines results of image and behavioral analyses
- Accepts inputs from third-party systems (account scoring, balance, and age of account)
- Prioritizes review to focus on highest-risk items

Charting a Course to Enterprise-wide Fraud Monitoring

Check fraud detection is one component of an enterprise-wide fraud prevention framework. Combining check fraud detection capabilities with other product- or channel-specific fraud solutions enables financial institutions to leverage the collective fraud activity and helps them rapidly identify fraud that is moving across channels or products.

Financial institutions across the country are beginning to recognize the tremendous benefits made possible by applying fraud prevention analytics in a holistic manner. An enterprise-wide fraud monitoring vision allows financial institutions to recognize patterns of fraud and use the intuitive nature of the solutions to assist in identifying fraud in other areas. Taking an integrated approach to managing fraud will help financial institutions achieve a three hundred and sixty-degree fraud monitoring view of consumer financial services.

Financial institutions are moving beyond the reactive fraud response and linking to enterprise risk management, regulatory compliance, and anti–money laundering solutions. Monitoring for fraud with a single, interconnected view moves financial institutions to enterprise-wide fraud management covering all product lines.

You may distribute tens, hundreds, or thousands of checks each month. Regardless of the number, you want to ensure that the checks clearing your account are legitimate and not the creation of fraudulent individuals. FIS's solutions can help you to more quickly identify fraudulent checks and safeguard against losses.

Leveraging Predictive Analytics and Models in Monitoring Deposit Activity

Traditional detection products are rules-based and require the risk manager to cast a very broad net to reel in the fraud. While this approach can identify a good percentage of fraudulent activity, the pool of alerts also includes a high number of false positives. This causes the investigator to work in a rush mode, resulting in missed fraud or often not finishing the review of all alerts. The purpose of this section is to present the best new approaches that demonstrate how deposit fraud can be effectively identified while simultaneously improving workflows and optimizing resources.

Predictive Analytics and How They Can Be Deployed?

Predictive analytics can be achieved in a variety of methods such as statistics and database mining. In deposit analysis, a predictive model is developed by taking a transaction set for a period of time in which the good and bad activity is known along with customer information for the same period of time. When strong predictive patterns or relationships are identified, predictive variables are created and can be used in a model to monitor future activity for similar good or bad patterns.

While predictive models are highly effective, a great solution will also provide the risk manager with a set of rules that can be layered in with the predictive models in order to give control into specific situations in which the model may not accommodate. Often, a financial institution may have policies to adhere to, or specific situations will always need to be reviewed. For example, some policies may require all items over a certain amount to always be reviewed. While a model may analyze and score the item with a low probability of fraud, the policy may still require a set of eyes to review. Simple rules to accommodate this situation should be available to the risk manager to set and change as needed.

When good activity and bad activity models are combined, the result is often a solution that effectively identifies highly suspicious activity that merits further investigation while also dismissing good activity, resulting in lower false positives.

It's All About the Data and How It Is Used

Traditionally, in terms of deposit fraud systems, most solutions look at:

- All-Items-File (AIF) contains debit and credit transaction details (deposit, withdrawals, cash in and out tickets, GL tickets, and so forth).
- Customer Information Files (CIF) contains customer-level information (name, address, telephone, social security number, and so forth).

Often missed with these two foundation files is a synergy between the risk of the item and the risk of the account holder. The item will have a score range from high to low. The account holder also presents a risk in terms of the ability to cover a return. For example, you may have a medium risk item that has been deposited into an account that currently does not have funds available to cover a possible return. In some cases, the investigator may place a Regulation CC hold to protect the institution. In some cases, the investigator may look at other accounts. The customer has to make a final decision. This is often a cumbersome task requiring inquiries to multiple systems. A good fraud prevention solution will systematically identify related account and provide this information to the investigator for expedited review. In the above example, if the medium-risk item went into an account with a low balance and the client also has multiple accounts with a high relationship balance, then the decision may not require a hold. A great fraud prevention solution will leverage strategies that enable the institution to auto-decision transactions and avoid creating the alert. This maintains high level of customer service while also preventing suspicious activity alerts unnecessarily

Hot Files

Institutions are often aware of certain transit items that present a high level of risk. This is often due to the historical experience such as known fraudulent activity, high NSF/UCF returns, and so forth. A transit item hot file is a very simple approach to house this transit item information. As items are processed each day, a hot file is checked for matching RT/account numbers and associated reason. Matches can result in an alert and presented to the investigator.

Safe Files

In the day-to-day process of managing a fraud prevention unit, it is common to see certain transit items on a regular basis. When these items often result in alerts, they are often simply recognized as a known good account and simply passed over for fraud review. This information can be housed in a safe file, and subsequent alerts can be suppressed from fraud review.

Hot files and safe files are effective in targeting high-risk items while also reducing false positives. These low-tech files can greatly improve efficiency

Return Deposit Items (RDI File)

On a daily basis, financial institutions receive a return deposit item (RDI) file that contains items previously deposited that the paying institution returned. There are a wide variety of return reasons that are important to the fraud/risk analyst. Return reasons such as account closed, counterfeit, forgeries, unable to locate, and NSF are very predictive in a fraud prevention model and quickly identify when these items reappear in subsequent deposits. RDI files should be aggregated over time to identify fraud patterns be provided to a statistician for inclusion in the model.

FDIC Special Alerts and OCC Alerts

Financial institutions may voluntarily report compromised instruments such as cashier's checks, money orders, teller checks, and so forth to the FDIC and OCC . These reports are made available to institutions in the event that the compromised items appear at their institutions. Descriptions of bad and good items are contained in the alert and can be leveraged by the investigator should they appear in an alert.

United States Postal Money Orders

The United States Postal Service (USPS) updates files on a daily basis on compromised United States money orders. MICR line information is provided and made available to institutions. As USPS items are identified in the AIF, they should be compared to the USPS hot file, and matches should be reviewed for possible fraudulent activity.

The data and analysis described above should be part of an effective deposit fraud detection and prevention solution. As new data becomes available from either internal or external sources, there should always be a consideration regarding its value to the fraud prevention strategy. Over time, fraud patterns may change, resulting in the need for models to be retuned or rebuilt. New or continually refreshed data is critical to the systems analysis and statisticians to maintain an optimized strategy

Shared Data: Opportunities and Challenges

Institutions can further improve performance by sharing relevant information at the appropriate time. Shared information can provide the bank of first deposit an early insight into known issues and varying degrees of risk. Conversely, it could also be utilized to expedite funds availability, a goal all institutions are seeking. However, depending on the design, a shared model can create sensitive issues and challenges:

- There is a concern with taking a marketing advantage in an attempt to solicit customers away.
- In existing pay-to-play approach, the institution that contributes the most data is viewed as making money off other contributors that have smaller volumes.
- The inequity for pay-to-play causes medium and small institutions to step aside. This creates significant gaps in the data, which causes the consortium to make assumptions and estimates to fill the gap.
- There are missing opportunities in other channels. While check is the preferred fraud tool and will likely stay at the top, other channels are also tested. Additional attributes can be captured in other channels and offer opportunity for sharing and network analysis.

As payments convergence (payments hub) comes to fruition, we will see a newer open architecture that is conducive to data sharing. It will be crucial for all processors (in-house and third party) to plan for improved data sharing approaches that are appealing to all size institutions and touch on multiple networks.

Batch and Real-time Analysis

Legacy detection systems focused on monitoring deposit activity in a batch process. This has served institutions well over the years, but many changes in technology have been adopted. Deployment of Teller Capture, Branch Capture, Remote Deposit Capture, and Image-Enabled ATM continue to move to becoming the standard. Consumer capture and mobile banking are also starting to be offered. These new methods and points for a deposit to be submitted have resulted in faster clearing times as well as new opportunities to be anonymous and attempt fraudulent transactions. Coupled with this is pressure to make funds available sooner than in the past. These advances and changes have put additional pressure to identify potential risks at the point where the deposit is presented to the institution. Real-time and near real-time deposit analysis systems are overdue.

Real-time Analysis

This provides the opportunity to review the transaction at the point of presentment. If there are risks identified at this point, information can be relayed to the source for resolution before the transaction is accepted. The source, for example, may be a teller or a strategy deployed at an ATM.

It is common deposit fraud practice to deposit a bad check in the evening and then perform the subsequent withdrawal early the next morning. The true loss potential for the institution is on the withdrawal side. Once the money is gone, the chance for recovery is almost zero. A real-time monitoring system must also communicate with the back office investigative team as well as the alert management system. For example, when a check is presented for encashment at the teller window, part of the analysis should include, in addition to the on-us analysis, a check for open or un-worked alerts on the same account. When this situation is identified, either the teller or the investigator can be informed of this additional alert situation.

Near Real-time Analysis

Some institutions may prefer strategies that allow the deposit transaction to be completed before fraud analysis is performed. This maintains quick service in areas where lines can build and enables detection earlier in the business day rather than waiting for large batches to be processed in the evening. Points such as ATM, remote capture, and consumer capture may be best served with this approach. For example, when a deposit is made at an ATM, immediately after the transaction is complete, the fraud prevention system processes the information. When an alert is created, it can be routed to the appropriate department for review and subsequent actions. This can be leveraged to expedite funds availability on good customers and deposits while also taking earlier actions on suspicious activity.

Enterprise Fraud Management

The focus of this brief has been solely on deposit fraud. There is no intent to create a silo approach to deposit fraud, as this would bring the inefficiencies the industry has experienced in previous decades. The concept of an enterprise fraud management has been around for a few years, and the definition is getting closer to being defined and will continue to be refined. A few additional points to consider for an enterprise solution:

- A few established effective detection systems are well engrained in some institutions. These may be developed by other vendors or in-house. An enterprise solution should allow the institution to leverage existing investments and avoid a rip-and-replace approach.
- Effective alert management should enable the consolidation of multiple alerts to a single alert work unit. As alerts are generated across multiple systems, this single view will allow the risk manager to determine how alerts should be managed and worked. For the investigator, the single view gives a much broader picture of the customer, account, and transactions.
- Complex Event Processing (CEP) fits in well with enterprise fraud management. While there has been much discussion regarding multi-channel and cross-channel fraud, there has been a gap in how to effectively solve for it. CEP is designed to monitor events across

multiple channels, analyze it, and take subsequent actions in real time. For example, there is considerable concern with good customers being approached with lottery scams, employment scams, and a variety of Nigerian and Internet type scams. Basically, a bogus check is given to the account holder with instructions to deposit the check and then wire transfer a portion of the funds back to the fraudster. This is hard to detect for established customers as they may have a strong relationship with their institution and their activities may go unnoticed. CEP monitors these events across channels and days to uncover this type of fraud.

Closing Comments

Fraudsters will most often go down the path of least resistance. This is why check fraud continues to grow year after year despite some of the well-established fraud detection solutions. Simply put, check fraud is easy. New payment channels that provide convenience for consumers continue to grow market share across the country. When we look beyond the United States, additional payment channels may start to move into the United States as well. Consumer capture, mobile-to-mobile payments, and nontraditional businesses getting into the payments space create new avenues for the more sophisticated fraudsters to test for weaknesses. Once uncovered, they will exploit it until it is closed.

While the challenges ahead will continue to grow, it is important to keep these concepts in mind as you review your approach to fraud prevention and enterprise payment management.

CHAPTER FOURTEEN

LOOKING BEYOND ENCRYPTION TO STOP PAYMENTS FRAUD

LUTHER MARTIN, VOLTAGE SECURITY, INC

THE most common way to protect sensitive financial data is by using encryption. This provides good protection for sensitive information which results in lower levels of fraud, but this protection is limited by system-level issues rather than by the technology itself, particularly by problems associated with key management. Innovations promise to help overcome of these issues, making the technology an even better way to reduce fraud in the future.

The strength of encryption

Encryption is a fairly mature technology. It's understood to the point where national governments, the most cautious and risk-averse organizations in the world, routinely use it to protect their most sensitive diplomatic and military communications. There are also careful and precise definitions of encryption and the security that it provides that let researchers create rigorous proofs of the security of encryption algorithms and protocols, which has made encryption one of the few parts of information security with a reasonable claim to being a science rather than a black art. The combination of sound theoretical foundations and many years of practical experience in its implementation makes encryption an ideal technology to use to reduce payment fraud.

The level of security provided by encryption is actually hard to understand because it involves numbers that are so much bigger than the ones where our intuition works well: although a 128-bit key doesn't sound that big, the number of possible 128-bit keys is extremely large. If an attacker has to try all of those possibilities to see which one is the key that he needs, he's extremely unlikely to ever succeed.

Back in the dot-com era, the Electronic Frontier Foundation built the DES Cracker, a special-purpose computer designed to beat the DES encryption algorithm. They managed to do this for only $250,000, showing that technology had advanced to the point where an attacker with a fairly modest amount of resources could defeat the now-obsolete DES encryption algorithm without too much trouble. The DES Cracker could test roughly 92 billion keys per second on 1,536 special-purpose chips. Given a plaintext-cipher text pair, the overall machine could try all possible DES keys in slightly more than nine days, and on average would find the key that decrypted the cipher-text in about half that time, or about four and one-half days.

Technology has made considerable progress since the dot-com era, and it's now possible to buy commercial off-the-shelf computers that are faster than the DES Cracker, although they're not actually that much more economical: the current state of the art gives you a machine that's five times more cost-effective, both costing less and having better performance than the older machine. Let's be wildly optimistic and assume that we can make a special-purpose computer that can test keys one billion times faster than the DES Cracker. Moore's law and http://www.technologyreview.com/read_article.aspx?ch=specialsections&s c=emerging08&id=20242&a= faster clock speeds can help us do this. Adding additional chips to our computer will also help.

But even with this implausibly-huge increase in computing power, such a hypothetical machine will still take roughly 100 billion years to recover a single 128-bit key. So unless a clever researcher finds an incredibly severe weakness in AES, it looks like that assuming that the protection provided by a128-bit AES key is essentially unbeatable is reasonable. On the other hand, it may be possible for a hacker to get sensitive information in a way that doesn't involve impossibly-huge amounts of computing power, and that's by finding a way to bypass the encryption altogether. .

Key management

A cryptographic key is much like the combination to a safe. If you have the combination, it's easy to open a safe, but it's hard to open one without the combination. But if a person is careless with the combination to their safe, a hacker can easily find it, and once they have it, the protection provided by the safe is essentially eliminated. Similarly, the keys that are used to encrypt data need to be handled carefully. If they're handled carelessly then the protection provided by encryption can be essentially eliminated. Key management covers all the details of how to handle keys carefully enough to ensure that this does not happen, and doing it securely is necessary for encryption to provide the protection that it's capable of providing.

While the chances of an adversary finding the right key that he needs to decrypt encrypted data are extremely unlikely, the chances of a mistake being made in key management are much greater. They're so much greater, in fact, that an adversary will almost never try to recover a key, and will try to find a way to bypass encryption instead. This principle is summarized in Shamir's Third Law, "encryption is typically bypassed, not penetrated," which Adi Shamir described in the presentation that he gave when we received the 2002 A. M. Turing Award for his work on public-key cryptography.

In practice, this means that we can essentially ignore the strength of the encryption itself. It's probably so secure that for all intents and purposes it's unbreakable. Weaknesses in key management and other system issues, however, will always be much easier to exploit, so they're where we should focus our attention if we want to understand how well sensitive data is really being protected.

What can go wrong?

Some of the problems caused poor key management are fairly easy to understand. In the common case where an application gets a decryption key from a key server, the requesting application needs to authenticate to the key server in some way to show that it's authorized to get that particular key. Managing the credentials needed to do this authentication can be difficult and expensive, so some IT organizations actually try to eliminate this step altogether by using no authentication at all, deploying a system where anyone, including any hacker, can freely get any decryption key that they request.

So while the encryption itself is still strong, its use in this particular way provides absolutely no security at all, and this weakness is caused by poor key management instead of weak encryption. Not being security specialists, IT organizations sometimes believe that if they are encrypting their sensitive data then they're complying with the relevant laws and regulations, even if they're doing it in a way that provides no meaningful protection to the data. Fortunately, this particular error is often caught before it is widely deployed, although it can sometimes be difficult for information security specialists to convince other IT staff that such a low-security solution really isn't a good idea.

Problems can also be caused if it's too hard to get decryption keys instead of too easy. If you can't get the necessary decryption key when you need it then your encryption process is really just a way to cryptographically shred your sensitive data, and a lack of confidence in key management seems to be a major obstacle to the widespread encryption of backup tapes today.

Industry analysts estimate that less than half of businesses currently encrypt their backup tapes, and that issues relating to key management are the most common reason for not doing so: they're concerned that they won't be able to decrypt an encrypted tape if they need to. Businesses apparently perceive this risk as being greater than the risk of losing a backup tape, so the reasonable decision is to not bother with encryption at all and to accept the risk associated with a tape being lost or stolen. Fortunately, this problem should be addressed soon. Interoperable products that implement the newest key management standards will become available over the next year or two will make it easy to do things that are either impossible or impractical today.

Other problems with key management are more subtle. An example of this is the weakness in the random-number generator that was used in the pre-2.0 versions of the Netscape browser. With an ideal encryption algorithm, one for which there's no known weakness, if cryptographic keys are generated randomly then they're all equally likely and an adversary has no better attack than to try all possible keys and check to see which of them is the right one.

But if keys aren't equally likely, the amount of work needed to find the right key can be dramatically reduced. A flaw of this very type in the design of the Netscape random-number generator actually reduced the strength of a 128-bit key down to only 47 bits, a level at which it's feasible to recover such a key using only a typical desktop computer.

Still other problems with key management are just caused by existing conventions. Existing standards, for example, typically require or strongly that encryption keys be generated randomly. This requires copies of the keys to be stored in a secure key archive because random keys can't be created again if they're needed. Such a system must also be extremely robust because if a key is lost then any data encrypted with the key is also lost, and that means that the key archive system is also very expensive.

Industry analysts project that at the current rate at which encryption is being adopted, that within 10 years systems that manage over one trillion keys, several terabytes of keys, will be in use. At that point, the cost of a secure archive for keys will be extremely high and a better alternative will probably be needed.

An alternative to generating keys randomly is to calculate any keys that are needed. The benefit to this approach is that a key that can be calculated once can also be calculated again, so there's no need to securely archive every key. This is a problem for which there is already a good solution, but one that has not yet been widely implemented. This involves the use of key derivation functions (KDFs), a technology that has been used in other cryptographic applications for many years. The derived unique key per transaction (DUKPT) protocol that is used to generate the keys used to encrypt PINs on POS devices is an example of this technology.

In a more general application, a key server can use a KDF to calculate a key from a per-key identifier plus a cryptographic secret that's known only to the server. The output of this calculation is the key that is returned to the requesting application. If that key is requested again, it is calculated again, so that it does not need to be securely archived. As the number of keys managed increases over the next several years, the more general use of KDFs will become more and more attractive, so the technology will probably see broader use in the future.

Summary

Encryption is hard because it involves arcane mathematics that's only understood by specialists. Key management involves technology, people and processes, so it's even harder to do well. Some key management problems are obvious and others are much more subtle. But because encryption is the best way to protect sensitive information, key management is a problem that we have to solve if we want to make the protection provided by encryption meaningful.

Innovations, like the evolving key management standards and the more widespread use of KDFs, will make key management easier in the future. Technology can solve some problems, but not all of them, and educating IT professionals about key management and why it's needed is just as important if we want to get the full benefit from using encryption to protect sensitive information. Strong encryption of sensitive information is definitely one of the best ways to stop payments fraud, but only if it's supported by equally strong key management.

Chapter Fifteen

Multi-channel Payments Fraud Management - A True Paradigm Shift in Fraud Detection and Management

Dena Hamilton, Norkom Technologies

A paradigm shift is happening in the world of payments fraud management. Gone are the days when financial institutions managed payments fraud on a silo'd, singular basis. Now with the realization that one fraud event can cut across multiple products and channels simultaneously, financial institutions are beginning to embrace a whole new way to manage the issue of multi-channel payments fraud effectively and efficiently.

Multi-channel payments fraud is a mounting problem for financial institutions the world over, stemming from the proliferation of evermore convenient multi-channel products and services offered by financial institutions eager to gain an edge on the competition. However, it would appear that convenience has a high price. Every new product, service and channel launched in the name of enhanced customer service creates a new doorway into the institution – a new risk to manage. For not only will customers cross the threshold of this new doorway, they will be shadowed closely by fraudsters – from the fraud opportunist to organized criminal gangs. Everyone will try their hand.

No payment type is immune from the risk of fraud. Indeed, fraud is capable of being perpetrated on virtually any payment device. Despite declining use, more fraudulent attempts are made on checks than any other payment type. Electronic payments, while a tougher challenge for criminals, are an increasingly growing threat. Databases, online information-sharing and increased access points enable criminal gangs to steal, buy and sell information to carry out fraudulent activity from the remotest corners of the globe. The introduction of third party internet providers has succeeded in adding an additional layer of complexity in the make-up of multi-channel payments and the lifecycle of fraud against it, with P2P (person-to-person) transactions and the availability of real-time and cross-border payments posing a particularly nefarious risk to financial institutions. What was once considered the 'safest' means in which to move larger amounts of money securely, wires are now enticing fraudsters the world over.

Globally, the financial impact of fraud is increasing. Fraudulent attacks and data breaches are costly, not only in terms of reputation and lost revenue, but also in terms of the administrative costs of restoring customer accounts and the associated regulatory reporting requirements. With the increased usage of internet banking and changing customer preferences driving the trend toward new and more flexible payment services, fraudulent attacks can be initiated from anywhere in the world, across all payment channels. Fraudsters are able to change their point-of-entry and mode-of-attack quickly. Together, the escalating number of coordinated fraudulent attacks, the rise in actual fraud losses, and associated regulatory and reputational costs are forcing financial institutions to re-evaluate and re-prioritize areas of improvement in fraud detection, investigation and resolution.

To create a successful multi-channel payment fraud monitoring and detection environment, financial institutions have to re-evaluate current practice in fraud management. This includes, but is not limited to, automated detection systems, collapsed investigation areas, multiple customer communication devices, and centralized compliance and fraud case management. There is a growing realization that fraud detection forms just one part of a wider end-to-end financial crime management program. What this end-to-end financial crime risk program looks like varies from institution-to-institution, however, we propose four tenets that should underpin all enterprise-wide multi-channel payment fraud management programs:

1. **Efficient Investigation**

   The past has shown us that a central case management system is not sufficiently robust when addressing this emerging world of multi-channel payment fraud. To meet the demands of this fast-changing environment, financial institutions need to deploy a typology-specific alert management solution that provides the applicable display and search screens, as well as the much required underlying workflow by varying fraud type. The most robust environment is one that reflects the concise depiction of the (1) origination – Channel, (2) transaction - Payment type and (3) initiation point – Customer. An "upstream" preprocessing function should be included that can incorporate all available information and can facilitate the identification of unknown links, minimize false positives and improve efficiency overall. These alert screens must also encompass an underlying workflow for the rapid review, identification and confirmation of fraud or no fraud. A powerful and robust case management tool is required to round the operational area environment. True end-to-end fraud management includes not only detection and investigation but prevention and governance of the financial institution's overall portfolio. The deployment of mass compromise analysis across ALL fraud channels, not just cards, provides the ability to find as yet unknown frauds related to the same location, employee, IP address, terminals, etc. Loss tracking and recovery enables the view of loss data to that of an alert level, pinpointing exactly the detection engines that are yielding the best results.

2. **Early Identification of Fraud**

   The effectiveness of most fraud programs can be measured using a few core metrics - how long before the fraud was identified, how much money was lost before the fraud was identified and how many accounts were impacted by the same type of fraud penetration. As financial institutions move from a silo'd to a multi-channel approach, the need for rapid identification becomes a matter of great importance. With real-time, online payments now a reality, coupled with the availability of multiple entry points into a financial institution and a diversity of channels, it is vital for financial institutions to become more nimble in their fraud detection.

The holy grail of early fraud identification is a solution that is capable of providing best-in-class detection, identifies fast-changing, multi-channel, organized attacks and generates a domain/channel-specific response. To achieve this, financial institutions should deploy multiple analytic tools to enable them to easily change models and their correlating risk-scoring parameters without having to undertake, and incur the cost of, a massive IT project. Specifically, financial institutions should be looking to deploy a Defense-In-Depth approach with multiple analytical techniques in a single, integrated multi-channel solution. The Defense-In-Depth provides the tools necessary to profile individual behavior, whilst also supporting the much needed multi-party and peer group analyses. Profiling can be leveraged in descriptive modeling and should be robust enough to provide rebuilds when necessary. A composite approach, where behavioral profiles and transactional data combined are used with a predictive mode, yields a higher level of performance in terms of false positive rate and fraud detected rate.

The era of the black box approach (utilization of statistical or neural modeling) to fraud detection is passing. The introduction of multi-channel fraud has demanded that the software industry provide its users with a completely transparent and tunable modeling environment, encompassing both the auto-pilot (black box mode) and/or a manual override (white box). The overall aim of this is to enable financial institutions to tune various model types "on the fly" to address changing threats without having to wait for vendor updates.

Financial institutions continually expand their own analytical departments - this has created the need for a set of analytical tools designed for the unique requirements of financial institutions. These include a Champion/Challenger capability for comparing the performance of different fraud detection models in live production; a smart mining and feature selection approach to intelligently identify attributes that predict fraud while removing redundant variables that serve no useful purpose; automated scenario suggestion that complements business rules designed by experts with scenarios that expose fraud patterns that are otherwise hidden in the data; and model management capabilities which ensure the performance of the detection system remains optimized. Essentially all these combine to provide a Risk Based Interdiction and Response Management **within** the transaction stream, moving from a simple block/release approach to a fine-grained strategy for responding in different ways to ever-changing fraud.

3. **Customer Communication**

   At one time, customer communication went through its own paradigm shift, specifically around the fraud detection dimension. While it was commonplace in the credit card environment to call customers when fraud was thought to have occurred, controversial debate was sparked when debit card usage and corresponding fraud levels rose. It was one thing to communicate to customers about a possible fraud attack on a fixed limit card, but when it's a fraud attack on customers' own funds, it became a far more sensitive issue to communicate. The debate centered on who would absorb the liability - the consumer or the institution?

   While the industry has moved past this debate, how the contact is made and the sensitivity surrounding the issue is still a priority. The biggest challenge today is to ensure duplicity in calls to the customer don't occur unless deemed absolutely necessary. Surveys show, banks that notified consumers of suspected or actual fraud immediately after the fact or as quickly as possible across multiple channels ranked better for customer service than those that didn't, improving overall cardholder confidence. Notifications over multiple channels were particularly significant, illustrating that it is important for banks to be able to alert customers of potential fraud with more than just a phone call.

4. **Consolidated View**

   The evolution to multi-channel payments is forcing financial institutions to review, evaluate and challenge themselves to combat the ever-changing landscape of fraud. A single, consolidated view is a necessary function of any modern day financial crime solution – one that goes beyond the highly touted 'enterprise' solution that simply enables a single system to look at payment types individually. Instead, a true single, consolidated view is an environment in which an institution may view customers' activities in a multi-channel, multi-product and multi-entity format. The viewing must be interchangeable, dynamic and configurable to meet the institution's specific business and operational requirements. It is only through this consolidated view that institutions will be able to achieve the ability to see where one fraud event has cut across multiple products and channels simultaneously. More importantly, only with this approach can institutions truly begin to identify the compromised channel and possibly prevent a greater attack against the institution.

Ultimately, the single, consolidated view of all customer payment activities is the cornerstone to achieving the much demanded end-to-end, multi-channel financial crime environment. It is this key piece of functionality that enhances the flexibility between the, oftentimes, diverse and segregated compliance and fraud investigation units, resulting in improved interconnectivity and resource management between the two disciplines. But above all, it is this single, all-rounded, consolidated view of customer activity that leads to the holy grail of early fraud identification and potential prevention of future frauds, enhanced customer communications, and finally, more accurate and complete reporting of suspect activity across multiple channels.

CHAPTER SIXTEEN

ADDITIONAL VIEWS

16.1

BEST PRACTICES: OOBA
AS A TOOL FOR SECURING PAYMENTS
PETER TAPLING, AUTHENTIFY, INC.

THE concept of employing "out of band" authentication (OOBA) is a technique that dates back to the Spartans in the 5th century BC. Basically, information send via a primary means of communication is validated or decoded via information send via a secondary means of communication. In modern Internet communication, the primary means of communication is the IP network, and the secondary means of communication is, well, anything else (e.g., not email, which still employs the IP network). In the early days of online banking, we all remember the ubiquitous "Thank you, we'll mail you a PIN" – where the postal service acted as the "out of band" communication channel.

E-commerce today cannot wait for a human courier, but the desire to validate messages – or in this case purchases – is no less evident. The telephone provides an OOBA channel for e-commerce which is available to all merchants and virtually all consumers. Telephone calls can be placed in true real time and the interaction coordinated with an active Internet session.

The telephone can be employed for OOBA via SMS messaging or via the voice channel (an actual telephone call). Voice telephone calls enable full interaction with the person involved in a transaction, and the success or failure of the OOBA process can be determined in real time. SMS messages are "store and forward", so the Internet application cannot know whether or not the message was successfully delivered. Both SMS and voice can be effective for specific purposes.

In a payments scenario, use of the telephone in this manner ensures the consumer can demonstrate control of a valid, working telephone number. According to the *CyberSource Online Fraud Report* ©2010 (CyberSource Corporation - www.cybersource.com), 1 in 4 e-commerce orders has been manually reviewed over the past 5 years. Further, the same study indicates that when orders are tagged for manual review, as much as 75% of the time the primary task for the reviewer is to contact the person placing or validate their phone number. Using OOBA via telephone can establish this contact during the Internet session in which the order is placed can at least make the manual review process much more efficient and may eliminate the need for the manual review.

Control of a telephone number can be confirmed using either SMS or the voice channel. Typically, some form of order confirmation code would be delivered to the telephone number in question, either via SMS or via a voice telephone call. The order confirmation code would then be captured via the web session to complete the order or payment process. If the OOBA process employs the voice channel, the order process can definitively determine if the order confirmation code has been delivered during the web session. SMS is "store and forward", so the order process must typically complete without the order confirmation code and a delayed process for accepting the code must be accommodated.

When employing OOBA, it is of paramount importance to validate and protect the telephone number(s) to be used. When a new customer relationship is being established, the telephone number entered by the consumer must be validated and risk managed. Calling the telephone number when it is provided is the most effective way to bind the telephone number to the registration/purchase event. Telephone number as a data element must then be treated as an important piece of personal information. IF the telephone number is to be used as an authentication mechanism, then controls must be placed over the ability to add or change telephone numbers for a given account.

OOBA benefits from layering of risk management techniques as much as any other approach. Is the telephone number being used on file? Can it be tied to the name/address in the order? Is there geo-location correlation between the phone number and mailing address? Has this phone number been used for fraudulent activity in the past? These combined approaches increase the effectiveness of OOBA.

Use of OOBA via the voice channel of the telephone enables interaction with the human being involved in the transaction. A variety of risk management capabilities become available with the opportunity to interact with the person involved in the transaction. Merchants can reduce disputes and charge-backs by confirming details of the transaction automatically via the telephone. Simple voice recordings are a valuable forensic and deterrence tool. Voice biometrics can provide strong authentication of returning customers and identify parties who have acted inappropriately in the past.

The OOBA process is a broad spectrum risk management tool. It can employ very simple confirmation processes for lower risk transactions, and engage the customer more deeply for transactions considered more risky. Robbers wear masks so as not to be identified. Bad guys do not want to be contacted by phone or leave a voice recording for the same reasons.

16.2
ANTICIPATING AND PREVENTING FRAUD IN THE WAVE OF MOBILE PAYMENTS
KNUD BALSLEV, FONWALLET TRANSACTION SOLUTIONS INC

The explosive growth of smart phones and the growing willingness of users to conduct financial transactions for goods and services via these devices means that the possibility of no longer needing to carry a physical wallet is quickly becoming a reality.

One of the major challenges of conducting any kind of financial transaction from the mobile devices is both the perceived and real threat of fraud. As this nascent industry develops, fraudsters are attacking every touch point within the ecosystem probing for weaknesses. Mobile banking has been a repeated target because it does not have the same security layers that PCs do leaving authentication-related issues as a major point of weakness.

By mid-2010, the mobile transaction segment is best described as very fragmented with multiple niche technology solutions seeking both the most convenient and secure solution for mass adoption.

These multitude solutions reflect that there are many ways to deploy mobile technology in and around an existing set of established processes for transactions. The main players include issuing banks, credit card companies and associations, mobile network operators, merchants, transaction acquirers, payment networks, prepaid service providers, wireless carriers, handset manufacturers and technology companies.

Point solutions typically directly reflect the interests of the company or organizations behind a solution. Examples include: one store/chain (such as Starbucks), one service (such as parking in a city), micro-payments for mobile content charged to phone bill, mass transit in one metropolitan area, etc.

When proposing authentication and authorization for any kind of transaction via a mobile device, the ultimate success with widespread usage will largely depend on whether it is implemented in such a way that it:

1. Prevents or minimizes fraud - through new and current best practices
2. Scales, to enable volume and payments across all payment interfaces
3. Works within the existing transaction ecosystem
4. Provides a superior user experience

This chapter is focusing only on the fraud aspects.

It is possible to take advantage of mobile technology, change the rules and achieve fraud prevention tools while at the same time as providing the convenience of using the mobile device to authorize payments:

A. **Out of band authorization** prevents man-in-the-middle attack:
    By using an additional communication channel (mobile) in addition to the internet protocol for eCommerce, man-in-the-middle attacks become almost prohibitively complicated. A hacker would have to compromise two different encrypted transaction streams simultaneously. Other targets will be easier to attack.

B. **Integrate with existing fraud detection and prevention solutions**:
    Banks, merchant acquirers, credit card companies and alternative payment means such as PayPal have extensive fraud detection solutions and a mobile solution should be able to add detection of threats in different ways complementing those existing systems.

C. **Use the location of the transaction to detect potential fraud:**

Most recent mobile phones have GPS, which will be able to provide a very good location-fix of the mobile device, which can be compared to location of a physical shop. In case there is discrepancy, appropriate default counter measures will be activated dynamically with additional security features.

D. **Minimize the exposure of critical, private and sensitive data**:
A healthy strategy for any implementation of mobile payment infrastructure should include means to eliminate any exposure of sensitive data. This includes avoiding storage of such data where not absolutely necessary. Preventing unauthorized access and fraudulent use can be greatly improved when sensitive data is simply not stored and otherwise not available to hackers as the threats from any attacks are greatly reduced.

E. **Be prepared when adding new payment methods:**
In the future there will be new ways to pay and the mobile devices will become a cornerstone for enabling most of these. It is critically important to implement solutions which have fraud preventions and protection built in.

Mobile transactions are rapidly becoming a reality. The advantages of safe authentication and authorization via mobile devices are measurable but the need to stay vigilant against fraud must be ongoing.

The goal of successfully launching mobile transactions can be achieved by using the best from established payment systems combined with carefully crafted new components. Oversight to guide critical aspects of the process are organizations such as Mobey Forum and FSTC in Europe and US, respectively, which have the role of coordinating work between the many parties involved, including the relevant regulators.

To insure mass adoption, the user experience must not suffer from the entire underlying infrastructure; it has to be easy to learn and easy to use for everyone and most of all it must inspire confidence that it is safe.

Contributed by FonWallet www.FonWallet.com

CHAPTER SEVENTEEN

Emerging Retail Payments Risk Issues: Perspectives from a Collaborative Dialogue

Clifford S. Stanford, Federal Reserve Bank of Atlanta

THE following are excerpts from the conference proceedings of an event entitled "Emerging Retail Payments Risk Issues: An Industry, Regulatory, and Law Enforcement Dialogue" hosted by the Retail Payments Risk Forum at the Atlanta Fed on November 5–6, 2009.

Note

The speakers' and other participants' views described herein reflect their personal views presented in the context of a working forum and do not necessarily represent the official views of the agency/organization with which they are associated. A full summary of the proceedings, additional presentation materials, and the results of polling questions asked during the event are available separately on the Retail Payments Risk Forum's Web site at www.frbatlanta.org/rprf.

Catherine A. Allen, chairman and CEO of the Santa Fe Group

Trust has eroded between consumers, financial institutions, and government. A continued loss of trust represents the ultimate emerging risk. Consumer and business memories will cause the trust recovery to lag an economic one. Simultaneously, financial services companies must adapt to an array of transformative new technologies presenting new opportunities and challenges. In this environment, public and private sector collaborative efforts are imperative to address emerging risks and to avoid unintended consequences of poorly informed policy choices.

Further, while we are reevaluating regulation of financial institutions, there are an increasing number of non-regulated firms competing in the financial services sector, such as person-to-person (P2P) lenders and even traditional brick-and-mortar merchants. Moreover, we are witnessing an evolution in technology portending dramatic change for financial services itself and introducing new risks, in particular, arising from social networks and anything mobile. How will liability for losses be allocated among the various parties involved in a mobile payments transaction?

Despite a challenging overall picture, there has perhaps never been a greater opportunity for transformative thinking. For example, firms should take a holistic cross-channel approach to risk issues that puts customers in the role of a trusted partner to help fight fraud.

Emerging Payments Market Developments: Trends and Risks

Cynthia Merritt, Atlanta Fed

Continued investment in innovation is driving the development of new payment devices and channels despite the economic downturn. This creates new choices for consumers and businesses and drives efficiency improvements overall, but may also introduce new challenges and risks for which stakeholders may be unprepared.

Contactless payments using microchips and near field communication technology, mobile phone–enabled platforms, and social networking platforms were noted as areas to watch. While slower to take hold in the U.S., the growing ubiquity of cell phones in developing countries has encouraged a rapid adoption of mobile phones for person-to-person (P2P) payments, remittances, and the use of stored value on phones for the purchase of goods and services. Social networks are emerging as potential payments intermediaries, particularly for small-value payments in ecommerce. For example, both Facebook and Twitter have permitted third-party developers to provide payment applications on their service platforms.

Marianne Crowe, Boston Fed

A range of factors are influencing payments markets, including a continued shift to electronic payments (noting a lag for business-to-business payments), increased non-bank competition, increased use of Internet-enabled payments, shifting demographics, changing consumer and merchant preferences, technology advances, emerging risks, and new regulation. Recent data and the Federal Reserve's most recent (2007) retail payments study have shown debit cards as the fastest volume growth category, displacing cash, checks, and credit cards at the point of sale. Debit card products include signature- and PIN-based models, but also are evolving to include innovations like decoupled debit cards, prepaid card models, and contactless technology. Newer developments also include virtual, single-use debit card numbers, and floating PIN-entry pads for Internet-based debit card transactions.

More consumer bill payments are moving online, due in part to consumers' increasing comfort level with this environment and its convenience, a positive sign of value in a banking product. More broadly, the opportunity for increased Internet-enabled payments remains huge, although the current economic situation has temporarily resulted in negative growth in online sales.

Alternative payment methods span multiple models provided through a wide variety of online payment service providers. The P2P payments market is an area to watch for innovation. The Fed's 2007 retail payments study found that 6.6 percent of checks (206 million items) paid in 2006 were consumer casual or P2P checks. This segment is currently dominated by independent service providers such as PayPal. However, the success of online banking is beginning to drive interest in bank-enabled P2P systems. In addition, mobile is postured as a feasible channel for P2P payments.

Most large banks in the U.S. today offer some form of mobile banking, permitting customers to check balances, receive alerts, pay bills, or transfer funds among accounts. There is a range of analyst predictions of strong growth in U.S. mobile banking going forward. However, there has been less traction in mobile payments, where the phone is used for purchasing goods and services. Obstacles to mobile payments growth in the U.S. include a lack of technology standards for interoperability, regulatory gaps, unresolved liability issues, and concerns with security, privacy, authentication, and fraud. A business model encompassing customer ownership, support, and revenue sharing must be developed where the mobile payments customer is shared by a bank and a telecom carrier. Finally, there is an overarching need for consumer education to influence demand.

In this evolving environment where new non-bank players will continue to enter the payments space, the risk attributes are changing and not well understood. Consumers are faced with many payment choices and may be unclear about benefits and risks, so consumer education and collaboration among payments stakeholders is needed to ensure a safe environment.

James Van Dyke, Javelin Strategy and Research

While we must always be attentive about what could go wrong in the emerging payments environment, we should not let our fears cause us to ignore positive opportunities. In particular, new technologies and payments models offer opportunities to partner with the customer, empowering them to offer better control over customer data and help prevent threats such as identity fraud.

According Javelin research, overall identity fraud has increased in the U.S. in recent years to as much as $48 billion of losses in 2008, touching all payments channels, even while average fraud amounts and costs to consumers have declined. The nature of fraud is changing, and fraudsters are moving faster, although low-tech methods are still common. Security and fraud represent significant drivers of new technology expenses, and security is the key driver of consumer choice of payments products. A good deal of fraud is friendly with one in ten victims able to identify the perpetrator. Javelin's research found that fraud was four times higher among data breach victims than consumers at large, but consumers have a poor understanding of their risk following a data breach despite receiving notice. Further, this lack of understanding may be increasing the time to detect fraud and causing higher out-of-pocket costs.

Mobile finance introduces complexity and risk, but also creates new opportunities for authentication via the handset and mobile network operators. A key error of the past has been the failure of the industry to partner with the identity holder to protect his information, which limits the effectiveness of security efforts while excluding relationship-based profitability benefits. Going forward, a reassessment is needed of the roles that companies and individuals play with regard to protecting identity records and the sharing of fraud costs, which can lessen the overall impact of fraud for everyone.

Data Breaches in Payments Systems: Roles and Best Practices for the Public and Private Sector Response

Brad Beytien, Federal Reserve Board

Data breaches are precursors to payments system risks. These threats are being publicized, and related alerts are being provided to banks, but the techniques involved evolve constantly and quickly. Given the increasing instances of payments fraud, some commentators have begun to question the efficacy of the current customer authentication standards deployed across the industry. Others have suggested that these exposures could threaten the viability of smaller banking institutions, particularly in cases where institutions have outsized payments businesses relative to their capital.

Jim Devlin, Office of the Comptroller of the Currency

There is a public/private sector framework, known as the FBIIC-FSSCC Cyber Security Committee, whose mission is to work with the financial services sector to strengthen cyber security and the resiliency of the sector's current and future IT operations. Their objective is to create a shared view of cyber threats by leveraging federal government resources. Among other activities, the committee develops and executes cyber security exercises to identify risk issues with the latest exercise, known as Cyberfire, accomplished in September 2009 and involving over ninety different organizations. The committee is developing a framework for improved information sharing, including by gaining security clearances for over one hundred critical private sector individuals. The committee's current interests include mobile devices and international telecommunications infrastructure. Included in the committee's long-range efforts is a financial services sector threat matrix to help focus future collaborative efforts, working with organizations like SANS, U.S. CERT, and the FS-ISAC. Top threats today include identity theft via malware, loss of telecommunications, and threats from insiders.

Don Rhodes, American Bankers Association

Corporate account takeovers are perhaps a logical extension of criminal activity using phishing and other such techniques. Phishing is the criminally fraudulent process of attempting to acquire sensitive information such as user names, passwords, and credit card details by masquerading as a trustworthy entity in an electronic communication. While phishing attacks are sometimes targeted espionage on key individuals who may have large accounts (spear phishing or whaling), fraudulent access to non-consumer accounts is attractive to criminals because one successful breach can result in major financial gain. To illustrate the point, Rhodes described the Zeus Trojan/keylogger malware, citing a 2009 case in Kentucky where a county treasurer's credentials were compromised, allowing criminals to log into county bank accounts from the treasurer's computer. The Zeus malware can be loaded just by opening an e-mail, which is usually targeted to treasury management staff and may draw attention by looking official, like a fake subpoena. In the Kentucky case, similar in nature to many other recently reported cases, funds were transferred in increments of less than $10,000 from the compromised account to mules established as fake county employees, who were recruited by the fraudsters via work-at-home job Web sites. These mules kept a portion of the funds and sent the remainder via non-bank money transfer systems to accounts in the Ukraine. In the Kentucky case, the county lost over $415,000 to this fraud. This and numerous other similar cases have been uncovered in 2009 by the *Washington Post*, which recently reported FBI estimates of $40 million in actual losses from similar attacks in recent years.

Awareness is critical. Businesses need to understand what data is the most sensitive, know where it resides, and assess controls according to the risk. Some have suggested practical steps specifically to address the corporate account takeover threat such as using a stand-alone computer with a non-Windows operating system and no e-mail capability to access business accounts online.

John Carlson, BITS

BITS sponsors, along with the FSSCC, an array of security, fraud, vendor management, and regulatory compliance activities, including outreach to academic, technology, and government communities to improve the resiliency of the financial services sector, including:

- Public/private partnerships among financial institutions, third party (non-bank) payments providers, and law enforcement to address payments fraud and cyber security threats
- Initiatives to improve Web security and ongoing engagement with the Internet Corporation for Assigned Names and Number (ICANN)

concerning a proposal to establish new generic top-level domains that could include domains that have finance-oriented names

- Development of e-mail authentication protocols to reduce spam and the transmission of malware through e-mails
- Surveys on current authentication practices of financial institution customers, employees, and business partners
- Expansion of the BITS Shared Assessments program, which helps financial institutions more efficiently oversee third-party providers

In 2010, BITS plans to focus on cloud computing and the security effects of social networking technologies and consumer behavior. There are also discussions with senior White House officials on strategies to improve identity management and a proposed research project to establish a financial services subnet within government-controlled domains to enable experimentation with strong B2B and B2G authentication technologies.

Law Enforcement Perspectives

Jay Lerner, United States Department of Justice

The Fraud Enforcement and Recovery Act of 2009 includes key provisions relevant to financial frauds. The Payments Fraud Working Group, an interagency group representing law enforcement, financial regulators, and other agencies seeking to improve information sharing and awareness of payments fraud trends and issues. This working group was one of the ideas that emerged from a 2008 event sponsored by the Retail Payments Risk Forum. The Justice Department has ongoing work to address cyber threats and related frauds.

Andrew Bonillo, United States Secret Service

Efforts to promote trusted collaboration among government agencies and with the private sector are critical to address cyber crime. Fraudsters are sharing information in sophisticated ways already, such as Web forums, so it takes dedicated efforts to keep up. Criminal hacker activity now is about stealing money, not about ego-tripping. Personal and payments-related data such as card information has become a commodity on the black market. In some sense, privacy protections for consumer information can be at odds with effective enforcement, and the fraudsters know this. Further, as soon as industry adopts a standard, such as end-to-end encryption of payments data, hackers will be trying to break through. These kinds of security measures may serve to shift civil liability, but they will not deter hackers for long.

The Secret Service is partnering with technology firms to understand emerging issues and technologies, including, for example, social networking sites. Law enforcement has a thirst for data on an ongoing basis to help with its efforts, even if it is old data, citing examples where such data has been helpful to spot signatures of fraudsters in investigations emerging years later.

Michael McKeown, FBI

The FBI is working through a public/private partnership known as the National Cyber Forensics Training Alliance (NCFTA) to develop new means to track and investigate account takeover frauds. The FBI is investigating money mules, and the FBI recently issued an alert on the issue. In this regard, the FBI is going after all cases and not just the high-dollar cases. Through the NCFTA, the FBI is working with the U.S. CERT group at Carnegie Mellon University to analyze the Zeus malware and provide law enforcement with intelligence for their work to address this problem. The FBI has had a number of successful investigations, including the DarkMarket carding forum sting.

Law enforcement does want to know about cases where there was attempted fraud but not losses. Suspicious activity reports (SARs) filed by financial institutions are actively used by law enforcement to detect trends and accomplish investigations, for example, to help identify money mules. While Zeus is the biggest problem currently, tomorrow's vulnerabilities may come in the areas of telecommunications and social networking. We can expect old-school exploits on these emerging delivery services for payments.

Industry Perspectives on Emerging Risks and Public/Private Engagement

Jane Larimer, NACHA

NACHA seeks to monitor and respond to ACH risk events in such a way as to minimize the long-term effects on consumers and financial institutions. ACH network volume has grown for many years as usage has expanded into new forms. NACHA has increased its attention on risk and fraud mitigation, and, since 2001, the ACH network has experienced steadily lower rates of return for unauthorized ACH debit entries, a leading indicator of misuse of the ACH. This rate was at an all-time low of 0.04 percent for 2008. Larimer referenced anecdotal evidence to suggest this trend is correlated with a rising use of remotely created checks, which are less easy to monitor. This highlights a need for tools that can manage risk across all payment channels.

The 2009 Association of Financial Professionals Payments Fraud and Control Survey (AFP Survey) found that only 17 percent of companies that experienced ACH-related fraud attempts incurred actual losses. Those organizations who incurred losses likely failed to adopt best practices, such as debit block tools and ACH Positive Pay.

Corporate account takeover schemes in which fraudsters gain online account access and send funds transfers via ACH credits and wire transfers to accomplices are of increasing concern. The ACH network may be facing a paradigm shift to a focus on unauthorized ACH credits, where monitoring is more challenging and there is insufficient benchmarking data. NACHA works with law enforcement and regulators to communicate risk issues and best practices to financial institutions and others in an effort to preclude future fraud schemes.

Dan Miner, Treasury Strategies

Financial institutions must consider over one thousand different standards in the payments legal and regulatory context. This burden is made more complex as financial institution risk management, and compliance efforts are fragmented by the product type with their own management structures attached to separate profit centers. There is often no central repository for information about risks affecting an institution, which can foster a lack of consistency in risk management, ineffective governance, and poor compliance.

Considering the risk to businesses from payments fraud, businesses should take greater responsibility for their accounts and make better use of bank monitoring services, third-party tools, and internal controls. Businesses are not taking full advantage of available tools like Positive Pay and debit blocks. Businesses should reduce the number of bank accounts used, monitor them daily, and reduce or even eliminate check payments, particularly given the persistence of check-related fraud as seen in the AFP Survey. Time-tested practices such as ensuring operational dual controls and segregating duties still have value as well.

Rue Jenkins, Costco Wholesale

In terms of outbound payments to suppliers and service providers, while check usage does persist, Costco has increased significantly its use of the ACH. On the inbound side, Costco has limited credit card acceptance for Visa and MasterCard. In the alternative payments area, Costco is now accepting payments online via eBay's BillMeLater service, is piloting a closed-loop PIN debit/ACH card product in Puerto Rico, and is exploring other point-of-sale alternatives.

The 2009 AFP Survey reported the highest amount of attempted or actual fraud in checks. Even while check volume is declining, the survey found that median fraud loss to businesses from checks rose from 2007 to 2008. Fraud attempts on merchants are hard to monitor, so constant corporate/bank communication is required, and education of staff is increasingly critical. Costco views payments breakdowns as reputational risks.

Conclusion

It is paramount that the payments industry, regulators, and law enforcement all seek to work together to understand, mitigate, and deter risks and fraud in the emerging payments environment. Clearly, further work remains to be done, and the landscape is ever changing. But the challenges faced are common to all parties, presenting an imperative for common understanding, information sharing, and collaborative action.

More of the results of the Atlanta Fed's Retail Payments Risk Forum event can be found on its Web site at www.frbatlanta.org/rprf.

Chapter Eighteen

Counter-Tsunamis "Future Think" on Extreme Countermeasures

James D. Pitts

THE water is rising. Shall we tie life boats together or build an ark? Many are in the water already and many, many more will be. I'd say we should consider doing both!

When I'm driving projects for the FSTC/Financial Services Roundtable I often ask my team to keep an eye out for the "big ideas." What I'm saying is, "Let's stay focused on the tasks at hand and get the job done, but not get so caught up in the details that we miss the comprehensive solution." These big ideas are often cloaked in the absurd. They may not seem to make good sense. They may appear to be impossible, or just the opposite—so simple or obvious that they can't realistically be the solution or someone surely would have already implemented them. You've almost got to believe in holy grails and silver bullets to find these ideas. Then you've got to accept the fact that a big idea may not be adopted until you throw it away and someone else picks it up and fixes it into something that really works.

We are a species that thrives on big ideas. We have a history of discovering cures for deadly disease by manipulating organisms so tiny that we can't even register them using our natural senses. We've built structures that we don't even know how it was possible to engineer. We invent machines that are many times stronger, faster, and maybe even smarter than we are. We travel distances and speeds that we can hardly comprehend. We analyze time, space, and other dimensions that we only know of through mathematical analysis and theoretical laws of physics. We definitely have the ability to reach out for and capitalize on "big ideas."

With all of that said, let me invite you to go on a bit of a scavenger hunt with me in search of a few big ideas.

Here's an example:

Airlines have had a couple of ongoing issues (as of the time this book was birthed). One is a really big one—security, and the other is more about process and business—luggage. You can tackle these issues up close or step back and look for a big idea. You can address them individually or look for something that addresses both.

"Up close" on the luggage issue could be a policy of charging for baggage checked to increase revenue. It could otherwise be a policy of charging for carry-ons to increase revenue *and* streamline departure.

"Up close" on the security issue has meant heightened security, increased hassle, and reduced customer service for all passengers. It has also required huge investments in technology that provides only partial solutions based on consistently perfect human management of the process.

Now step back.

The big idea for the luggage issues might be charging for **all** luggage to increase revenue, but charge more for carry-ons and less for baggage checked to also address streamlining departure. Another angle of course, could be to invest in advertising that *luggage flies free* to gain market share via irritated passengers changing carriers.

The big idea for air travel security might be to give passengers an extreme choice.

1) For those more concerned about economics than about the remote odds of being victimized by a malicious attack (let's face it—most likely murdered), they may choose to fly under the current limited restrictions.

2) For those willing to perhaps pay a bit more for near "zero defect" security (complete separation of risks) at five to seven miles up (We're talking about your life; why not go to extremes?), it could be appropriate to consider offering separate flights for luggage and humans. Under this scenario the passengers may only board with cloth (clothing) and paper (personal reading). Any other accoutrements

could be supplied on board (food, pens, videos, web access). The extras could generate revenue or not; you're likely already commanding increased booking and per-flyer revenue. Incidentally, you've also resolved the luggage issue with this option.

Absurd? Maybe. Certainly, there are a lot of arguments for the lack of practicality of such an offering. For now, we'll just float it. It may get picked up, thrown away, or spark the idea that really makes air travel attack proof, luggage handling effective, and running an airline profitable.

Have you gotten the gist of looking for big ideas? OK then, let's explore a few big ideas about tying life boats (conceivably practical fixes—improvements) and building arks (extreme stretch comprehensive solutions) To deal with this payments fraud tsunami.

Big Idea Counter-Tsunamis

There's been a lot of great "up close" and "big idea" thinking on stopping payments fraud already. In the war on payments fraud, the requirement for this type of thinking is continuous.

Some of the great "up close" thinking includes signature verification, certification mechanisms built into paper instruments, institutionally issued photo identification, as well as various automated verification practices.

Some of the big ideas have included PIN's (personal identification numbers) and passwords, smart cards (use of integrated circuit-chip technology), biometric identity technology, activity analysis, encryption, and tokenization to name a few. Even combinations (multi-factor authentication) of the above, such as chip and PIN (EMV) have proven to be big ideas.

I must say, however, I'm not sure all of these big ideas have been applied ideally. For instance—having an individual provide a self-administered finger print. Locks are for honest people, right? Like baby pictures. Not long ago I frequented a tanning salon that used digital finger print verification for access to tanning beds (as opposed to washable ink pads like several sophisticated banks use). Do you think there is any possibility that we'll someday feel the same way about providing such things to, uh—everybody—as we feel now about having provided social security numbers and other personal information to everybody a decade or so back? Oh well, I digress.

There are many "it's not good enough" battle cries these days. We're hearing observations repeated such as, "Privacy is no longer an issue. It doesn't exist. Everything about you is available on the internet," and "The signature is dead," or "The inconvenient PIN—who can keep up with all those numbers?" With these and others ringing in our ears, let's take a listen and push onward.

The Collaboration Counter-Tsunami (Group Wave)

Industry Stakeholder Convergence

Take a moment and think about the challenge of payment fraud prevention from a set of perspectives based on stakeholder management.

Consumers (payers) want convenience and security (to be held harmless). What a fraud-proof payment system requires—relative to consumers— is zero effort, perfect identification authentication.

Merchants (payees) want their money (now) without risk (with minimal or no cost).
Low cost, real time, secure transactions—live or virtual.

Governments want healthy commerce and taxes to cover costs. (Don't get me started.)
This will require an absolute identification and authentication system as well as a secure public data network system most likely funded by new taxes. Let's face it, private enterprise can only do so much.

Financial Institutions want no leakage (losses) and reasonable profits, which means security cubed that they can utilize without having full burden of funding. This might be interpreted as perfect authentication, data security and integrity, non-repudiation, all packaged in a convenient, low cost model.

This is an overly simplified short-list of top stakeholders. There are others to be considered and varying relationships to consider associated with various accounts, channels and payment types. To ensure that everyone gets what they want, certain essential stakeholders will have to converge and collaborate. The barriers may include things such as who calls the meeting, who's in charge, who gets to address their concerns first, who will listen, who will fund, and how do we justify this back to the folks in charge who don't attend this type of meeting? Okay, it's much, much, much more complicated.

There is a massive amount of collaboration that must take place within each payment type or channel. Whole industries grow out of associations, rules groups, and process improvement. In the end, complex systems, legal precedents, and agreements spread the cost and risk amongst the stakeholders. The problem is these groups each operate within their own silos. As payments converge, so must the organized, semi-comfortable silos converge into a larger and more collaboratively integrated group.

The Enterprise Matrix

There is another place where the stakeholders tend to live in silos—our financial services institutions. The massive nature of many companies and their merger and acquisition histories that help to make them so large, has created significant complexities involving effective internal coordination along with inconsistent updating or consolidating of legacy systems. This facilitates opportunities for the fraudsters (What a cute name for them. What are they, hippie elves?) to generate attacks across multiple product lines.

When you've consolidated multiple organizations that have independently invested significant capital into unique technology models, it's not always practical to convert all units onto the same platforms immediately. The process is tantamount to attempting to reconstruct several small ships into one large ship in the middle of the ocean. In this case, the correct approach is to better coordinate the fleet instead of building the mega boat. Though the fleet is somewhat disjointed, they all have certain things in common—lifeboats for instance.

For this analogy let's think of lifeboats as individual technologies that are all capable of doing their limited jobs, each playing a part to thwart different malicious threats. When lifeboats are in the water they have a tendency to drift apart. They may loose sight of each other. In a multiple lifeboat event it may be practical to tie the boats together. From a financial-services enterprise perspective, it may be time to tie the lifeboats together as well.

There are many effective individual technology packages that address different products, payment types, and attack methodologies. Effective systems integration might tie these together into a single managed system. This system matrix would generate effective cross-channel information and alerts to better address multi-channel attacks and minimize cascading damages. In an effective matrix the communication would flow and countermeasures would engage between silos as efficiently as might be expected in a single chain of command. In the big vision, this matrix might even automate suspect transaction traffic flow, diverting transactions flagged by fraud-monitoring modules through different technology review processes while comparing malicious activity across channels or product lines.

Really cool lifeboats such as some of those talked about throughout this book, might behave more like surfboards—whizzing around unfettered doing amazing things! Keep in mind, big ideas may take a long time to become real. We need to map the journey of what's happening today to what ideally may occur in the not-too-distant future.

Real-Time Communication

At the peak of my management career Star Trek reruns from all of the various series, including the original, were very prolific on late-evening television. As I succumbed nightly to my last e-mail fix of the day, I came to realize how many fabulous management principles were embedded in the shows. My history with Star Trek goes way back. You might say, "I was a Trekkie before being a Trekkie was cool."

For those of you with similar secrets in the closet, I'm sure the statement, "Resistance is futile!" stirs vivid Star Trek memories. This is the emotionless war cry of the Borg collective. You might call them a collaborative group of various species joined together by persuasive technology. The Borg (the bad guys in the show) had perfected collaborative communication. Unfortunately, they had also taken cooperative behavior to such an extreme that individual identity was lost. The other half of their familiar message was, "You will be assimilated!" I'm talking real identity theft, not just impersonation.

The incredible advantage the Borg had over their enemies was their ability to communicate with literally everyone in their collective (multiple disparate organizations and individual units) to coordinate efficient combined efforts to defeat (okay, and assimilate) all challengers in their path. This is real-time communication at its optimum. I'm not suggesting that we all hook our *iphones* into our central nervous systems and become *androids* (I don't know, ask me again in a few paragraphs—cybernetics may be fun!), but we do have incredible technology readily available to us to facilitate real-time communication. We just have to be assimilated … uh, get organized.

We're up against self-inflicted barriers again on this. There are regulations and laws about sharing information that are somewhat arduous. There is liability associated with getting it wrong. Generally speaking, most financial organizations aren't forthcoming with information that might cause embarrassment or loss of public trust. Most are not really even sure of what should be shared and with whom. There are always competition issues about providing too much help for the other guys. Who will fund collaboration, and who can we trust with the responsibility of coordinating the collaboration, not to mention the security of all the communiqués?

With all of that said, great strides are happening through organizations such as the FS-ISAC. We need to keep moving forward with a vision to connect all stakeholders (banks, law enforcement, merchants, government, corporations, consumers, and the like) as a single collective of need-to-know, need-to-coordinate organizations and individuals. However, this collective will not be like the Borg where everyone knows everything all the time, but where all of the various participants will know only what they need to know, when they need to know it to be an effective member of the overall collective. Ultimately, the working model will have to be designed with customized restrictions to facilitate appropriately formatted inflow of information consistent with regulations and views to only the information needed by the individual collaborators, as they need it.

In our twenty-four-hour-a-day world, real time information can be shared effectively with available technology if we are willing to commit to the right level of collaboration.

The Identity Authentication Counter-Tsunami (Next Wave)

This one is at the top of the list. In my mind, it may be the most important opportunity and likely must come first chronologically to truly secure the payments system against fraud. To start with (up close) let's assume there are various types of identities that need to be taken under consideration:

Original Identity or birth record – You know, the "little foot print" biometric. The challenge, of course, is that some of these get skipped, lost, or destroyed. They are also relatively easily manipulated to support identity impersonation.

Legal Identity – Social security number and/or government-issued picture ID (which is usually acquired based on a certificate of birth or reasonable alternative). I'm not aware of anyone scientifically comparing the big foot prints to the little ones as a requirement to get a government-issued ID.

Credit History – Financial-risk history identity based on behavior related to your known financial performance and typically associated with your (alleged) legal identity.

Biological Identity – Amazingly, each of us has unique, permanent, one of a kind, measurable biological characteristics that are conveniently with us always (usually).

Fake Identity – Can I just say that locks and identities (up to this point in the history of civilization) are mostly for honest people. Crooks are crooks because they can bust 'em up and fake 'em.

Let me summarize by saying that while our identity-tracking capabilities are some of the most effective the world has ever known, we are clearly in an identification crisis.

The best you should expect the financial services industry to do right now, is to manage credit-history identity supplemented by exception- or anomaly-based special handling. It's good that we know who most of the honest folks are. It's bad that we don't know who everybody is. It's very, very bad that we don't know who all of the dishonest people are. The good news for now is there are some very good efforts and techniques helping us manage the identities we can, as well as many of the anomalies.

Now let's step back. What is the ideal? We'd like to know who everyone is all of the time, with convenient and infallible authentication capability. This will require that everyone be registered, not necessarily at birth, and authentifiable (in a word) as a pre-requisite to conducting commerce (among other things of course, but I'm focused on payment fraud).

There are, at least, two major challenges:

1. Privacy issues and law – This level of identity means eliminating commercial anonymity or a portion of privacy for individuals conducting most legal transactions.
2. Potential identity fraud – It may be impossible to perfect mitigation for this, especially when it is digitized, but we can certainly do much, much, much better than we are now.

With the two challenges above, I submit the following assertions:

- Identity is a moving target with big feet/little feet, old name/new name, current address, new phone number, and so forth.
- The identity that each of us is most closely and permanently (relatively speaking) attached to is our biological identity.
- Biological identity can be authenticated via well-engineered biometrics, which are virtually (potentially, someday) infallible.
- Biometrics can be authenticated effectively utilizing a mobile, remote, always-present technology.
- Multi-factor authentication methodology can be used to effectively identify an individual.
- Biometric technology may be used to establish a "golden" or "most true" identity for every carbon-based life form in existence—certainly at least the human species. This identity could be the most consistently accurate, available, track-able identity possible—regardless of the other variables associated with the individual's existence.

I suggest the most effective, absolutely authentifiable (there's that word again, anyone have a dictionary?) identity possible in the near future might be a form of "tagging" by means of a cybernetic chip. To be clear, I'm talking about a chip implanted into its host. More durable, informative, convenient, and certainly more reliable then paper documents, ID cards, or identification numbers, this chip-based tagging could have an additional benefit of leaving nothing to the questionable observation of other humans.

Forget about ID-related thefts. No one can steel your thumb or eyeball, like in the movies, and use it to sneak into the top-secret laboratory or even to withdraw funds at a nearby ATM. Your chip (by requirement) will know it is definitely you standing in front of the ATM at a specific bank branch location, along with other important facts, such as that you're alive and well (whole) and even little anxious, because the ATM's response time is a bit slow.

Now let's strengthen verification and harden the target against ID theft with maximum (convenient, inexpensive) multi-factor authentication that I call "triangulation plus."

It takes three intersecting lines to locate or identify a point in space. But when there are more dynamics at play, you may need more identification factors to confirm identity correctly against a set of complex factors. To keep it simple, let's start with every reporter's mantra: who, what, when, where, why, how? Then let's build from there.

What can I verify with a chip?

Who – The individual I claim to be

What – Confirm multiple facts relative to the chip and biological specs of the individual (including state of health and psyche)

When – Confirm the time against the payment system's transaction time

Where – GPS verification of proximity to the payment terminal or device

How – Confirm payment types and accounts available based on CHIP information

(to be encrypted or tokenized)

Out-of-channel factors could then include more traditional elements such as behavior history and trends, valid terminal and merchant, PIN or password, mobile device communications, and so on.

The first social security cards were issued in 1936 amid much controversy. Newspapers ran stories that people would be required to wear dog tags and would be forced to complete questionnaires probing for personal information. Were it not for social security numbers being tied to the New Deal as part of the nation's efforts toward financial recovery after the Great Depression, they would likely not have been adopted or accepted.

This is not about 'Big Brother' or the 4th amendment. It's not about loosing individual identity or privacy. It is about establishing and securing individual identity in a proactive way to avoid criminal invasion of privacy and identity theft.

I stated earlier that we are in an identification crisis. Perhaps not everyone agrees we are yet in a crisis, but I suspect we will not update to a comprehensive approach to identity management without some form of crisis-related motivation or justification. How deep and wide must the tsunami get? Or what much more devastating event are we waiting for?

Secure Internet Counter-Tsunami (Web Wave)

I'm sure most of us have heard the internet referred to as the technological version of the wild, wild west or even the Oklahoma land grab. Visions of yesteryear mixed with fears of tomorrow. I remember my father sharing stories of childhood experiences with early automobiles (sheesh, I'm getting old!). There was not a lot of traffic in those days, especially in rural areas. Children were often allowed to drive, and there was a time when a driver's license was not required in many areas. It's hard to think of that today. The power wielded behind the wheel of an automobile is often lethal, especially with the traffic volume we have today. It's almost unimaginable to think of unregulated driving, and we have come to accept individual-freedom restrictions including speed limits, vehicle registrations, inspections, traffic laws, driver's-license requirements, and even seatbelts, as fully appropriate with proven positive results.

Our nearly global road system has proven to be one of the most effective advancements civilization has known. Economic and cultural success by most standards only truly exists in countries that have reasonably well-developed road systems, and most population centers would consider it completely unreasonable to have unlimited, unregulated traffic flow.

Similarly, the internet is one of the most effective advancements civilization has known. The roads go virtually everywhere, and anyone with a vehicle is welcome. The similarities are almost eerie. How much power does an internet user have, and what are the potential dangers? Should internet devices (vehicles) not be regulated and users (drivers) licensed, or at least known? Restrictions are evolving, but there are just a few cops trying to catch a whole lot of robbers. Again, enforcement is catch as catch can, much like automobile traffic policing.

Let's step back and look at the big ideas.

Licensing drivers and registering vehicles seems to be a positive in many ways.

Requiring vehicles to be appropriately modified with safety features seems to be very positive as well. Statistics confirm significant numbers of lives saved.

Sporadic police work helps, but why not be comprehensive?

What if every red light had a camera, and every vehicle or driver could be tracked via GPS? What if every vehicle were smart enough and otherwise equipped to obey traffic laws, and avoid collisions?

What if we could confirm, with an automated real-time capability, vehicle and driver identity, location, speed, red-light behavior, and so on?

We have the technology to do most of these.

I submit we should attempt to manage vehicular traffic better to save lives and thwart crime, while preserving all privacy except where it violates or threatens others' freedoms to life or liberty.

I further submit that we should manage internet traffic in a similarly aggressive fashion. In fact, the approach for internet regulation has almost been laid out (ok, I'm stretching the analogy) by the approach to transportation regulation. I suspect the rabbit hole goes even deeper in areas of similarity as we look at it harder. Practices are already evolving around white-listing legitimate traffic on the internet. A comprehensive approach to this should eventually take the form of regulation for the good of law-abiding society. Given the nature of the internet and the rapid development of technology, comprehensive near zero defect practices should be achievable, more readily even, than with our physical-transportation models.

Flys in the Ointment

With all my fanciful thinking regarding counter-tsunamis that could prevail against the ensuing payment-fraud tsunami, I clearly scribbled outside the lines of the current coloring books. There are at least a couple of recurring themes I would classify as serious barriers to progress on these visions. The two I'd like to comment further on, are privacy and funding, most likely tied to other holy words in our culture that seemingly get more confused every day. Please bear with me for a few more lines of print.

Privacy and Freedom (Common Sense Approach)

There are a few things in my life that I feel should be allowed to be private. By their very nature they are mostly things that know one else cares about and/or frankly has no business caring about. These can be very small things or very large things. I firmly believe these areas of privacy can, should, and will be protected in an appropriately functioning society. There are other areas of privacy that may be valued for some but are detrimental to society. These areas should be judged in terms of individual freedom versus individual freedom and alternative levels of participation in the benefits of organized society and potential consequences.

Freedom isn't absolute. There is a delicate balance between individual rights and the rights of others. Personal freedom ends at the boundaries of others' freedoms. Personal freedom should not support actions that harm others. It is generally acceptable today that there are no-smoking areas. There are also smoking areas. Both leave individuals the freedom to decide to what level they will participate in society. You also have the freedom to acquire unlimited assets (or not) subject to an appropriate transaction and most likely some level of taxation.

If I feel a driver's license infringes on my right to privacy, I may choose not to drive, or I may drive illegally and be subject to consequences imposed by society. There are stories of tribal cultures who believed photographs allowed photographers to steal their souls. If you don't want your picture taken in public stay home and order in, or move to the mountains (get season lift tickets).

No one should be forced to use the internet, but perhaps individuals who wish to enjoy the advantages offered by its use should be willing t support the balance of freedom between individuals to live within the secured walls and regulations of societies. There will continue to be gates, on-off switches, and alternative choices. Likewise, certain payment transactions may require extreme identification authentication. If you wish to be anonymous, bring cash or other assets and accept that you'll have a limited number of payee alternatives.

Funding and Taxation

For every action there is an equal and opposite reaction. You don't get a new car without someone paying for it. You can't build or manage roads without taxes. You can't travel the road safely without law enforcement.

When I was a child, I used to think cars were magic. They ran without peddling, and I road for free (Dad paid for the car). When I was a man, I used to think the internet was magic. Who funds all this stuff anyway?

Collaboration, identity management, and internet security will require significant change. Who will make this change happen? Who will fund it? The answer should appropriately be all of the stakeholders who gain from the existence of the programs and eventual securitization they provide. Ultimately, these things will require global collaboration, top-down regulation, and huge investments. Will we do the right things proactively or wait for something catastrophic to justify the need?

The answer for funding appears to be internet security-specific taxation, to finance managed comprehensive controls. Again, the only thing likely to create significant movement here quickly might be a crisis. For now, unfortunately, there are probably many who feel that taxes are a greater crisis than constant theft, or even predictable catastrophe.

I love my car, my PC, and my cell phone. I like roads with responsible drivers and safe surfing on the payments ocean. As far as I'm concerned they can call it a counter-tsunami tax, so we can all surf happily ever after.

Epilogue

I sincerely hope you've enjoyed the waves we've attempted to address in this volume of the Surfing Payment Channels series!

My intention was to generate some serious awareness of very real issues on the topic of payments fraud, expose you to some of the top leadership in the industry who have a view to the problems as well some realistic solutions, and finally, to titillate you with a little creative "stretch" thinking that may someday lead to ideas or inventions supporting large-scale corrective actions.

Hopefully, you've discovered some value in the read and the time you've invested.

I challenge each and every one of you to pick up your board and surf the counter-wave of your choice in the ongoing battle against the payments fraud tsunami.

CONTRIBUTOR BIOGRAPHIES

Richard Oliver, Executive Vice President, Federal Reserve Bank of Atlanta

RICH Oliver is an executive vice president with the Federal Reserve Bank of Atlanta and has been with the Bank since 1973. He is currently the director of the Retail Payments Risk Forum, working collaboratively with organizations across the payments industry to research and mitigate payments risk.

From 1998 to 2009, he was the payments product manager for the Federal Reserve System. In this capacity, he had responsibility for managing the Fed's check and ACH businesses nationwide. Earlier in his career, Mr. Oliver served as planning analyst, administrator of the Automated Clearing House, chairman of the Federal Reserve's Electronic Payments Implementation Task Force, manager and officer in charge of business development and check software, and staff director for the Federal Reserve System's Policy Committee for Financial Services. He also serves on the Federal Reserve Bank of Atlanta's Management Committee.

Mr. Oliver received a bachelor's degree in math from the University of Nevada, a master's degree in information and computer sciences from Georgia Institute of Technology, and an MBA in Management from Georgia State University. He has also completed executive development programs at Harvard University and the University of Tennessee.

William B. Nelson, President and CEO, Financial Services Information Sharing and Analysis Center (FS-ISAC)

Bill is the president and CEO of the Financial Services Information Sharing and Analysis Center (FS-ISAC), a nonprofit association dedicated to protecting financial services firms from physical and cyber attacks. Members within the FS-ISAC include organizations from banks, credit unions, securities firms, and insurance companies. The FS-ISAC fulfills its mission through the dissemination of trusted and timely information regarding physical and cyber security risks to its membership.

In 2009, Bill was elected vice chair of the ISAC Council, a group dedicated to sharing critical infrastructure information with the government and across the key sectors.

Before joining the FS-ISAC, Bill was the executive vice president of NACHA, the Electronic Payments Association from 1988 to 2006. Bill oversaw the development of the ACH network into one of the largest electronic payment systems in the world, processing nearly fourteen billion payments in 2005. He also oversaw NACHA's rule-making, marketing, rules enforcement, education, and government relations programs. Prior to joining NACHA, Bill held several treasury management and lending positions within the banking industry.

Larry Robinson, President, Armor Safe Technologies

The first eighteen years of his life were spent growing up in the mountains of beautiful Colorado. In these formative years he learned to work heavy construction with his family and pursued the normal boyhood activities of football, wrestling, skiing and hiking. He left home at eighteen to attend college. There he met his sweetheart and they have been married for nearly 34 years. Larry is the father of three wonderful sons, all of whom have worked in the safe business at some time in their careers. Two are presently still engaged in this endeavor and one is attending college classes in Abilene, Texas.

Larry Robinson is currently President of Armor Safe Technologies, located in The Colony, Texas. He has been in this position for over 10 years. Prior to entering the safe industry he was a 7-Eleven franchisee and restauranteur in the then small cities of Nampa and Boise, Idaho. He has held numerous positions in the cash controller (Smart Safe) industry since 1989. Products he has brought to market hold numerous patents.

Larry has a passion for bringing innovative ideas to the cash control market. His company motto is "Changing the Way the World Counts Cash."

Joe J. Gregory, Vice President of Marketing, Orbograph

Joe, vice president of marketing, oversees the strategic and tactical marketing activities for Orbograph, including the market initiatives for Orbograph check recognition, data mining services, and check fraud detection. Joe has been with

Orbograph for ten years and in the check processing industry for more than twenty years. He started in check processing at Wausau Financial Systems, Inc., holding a variety of positions including regional sales manager, director of consumer products, and manager of product management. In June 2009, Joe graduated from the University of Phoenix with an MBA in Marketing.

Robert Jones

Bob has more than thirty years of experience leading fraud risk management programs. A recognized leader in the financial services industry and a sought-after expert in risk management strategy, Bob has devoted his career to innovative financial services fraud reduction and risk management.

Today, Bob is a consultant, educator, and expert witness and serves as the principal of RW Jones Associates LLC. Until May 2004, he led FleetBoston Financial's operating risk management programs and chaired Fleet's Operating Risk Committee. He joined FleetBoston in January 2000 after a twenty-one-year career with KeyCorp, where he was responsible for all fraud detection and prevention systems and programs.

While at KeyCorp, Bob was instrumental in reengineering the company's corporate security function to establish an innovative, customer-focused approach to providing security services. This program demonstrably enhanced the quality of the delivery of security services while materially reducing expense, and it was featured in a 1995 issue of *Security*. Bob also investigated and assisted in the prosecution of significant bank fraud cases, including the $1.1 billion Phar-Mor case.

Bob is deeply committed to contributing to the well-being of the larger financial community. He is the former co-chair of the BITS Fraud Reduction Steering Committee and former chairman of the American Bankers Association's Operating Risk Committee. He has also served as chairman of the Financial Institution Fraud Committee of the Association of Certified Fraud Examiners.

Bob is an adjunct professor at Utica College, where he teaches in the master's program in economic crime management. His articles have appeared in the *RMA Journal* and the *Journal of Economic Crime Management*.

Bob earned his bachelor of arts degree from Capital University in Columbus, Ohio, and his master of science degree from Utica College.

Ori Eisen, Founder, Chairman, and Chief Innovation Officer, 41st Parameter

Ori is the founder and chairman of 41st Parameter. He has spent the last ten years in the information technology industry and is respected for his business knowledge and leadership. His background includes an in-depth application of innovative solutions for preventing business to consumer e-commerce fraud.

Prior to launching 41st Parameter, Ori served as the worldwide fraud director for American Express focusing on Internet, MOTO, and counterfeit fraud. During his tenure with American Express, Ori championed the project to enhance the American Express authorization request to include Internet-specific parameters.

Prior to American Express, Ori was the director of fraud prevention for VeriSign/Network Solutions. By developing new and innovative technologies, he skillfully reduced fraud losses by over 85 percent in just three months.

Ori has an extensive background in developing system infrastructure and implemented solutions, and he is highly regarded in the information and payment technologies industry as a noted leader and technology innovator. Based on this reputation, industry insiders often quote him, and he receives numerous invitations to appear as a keynote speaker for industry events and conferences.

Ori holds a bachelor of science degree in business administration from Montclair State University.

Michael Milgramm, Inventor and CTO, IdentaZone Inc

Michael Milgramm currently serves as Executive Vice President, and Chief Technology Officer of IdentaZone Inc., responsible for the company's strategic development in the area of innovative biometric solutions. In this role, he owns technology strategy and IP strategy for the company, and is responsible for coordinating advanced research efforts for industry-leading biometric security products.

Mr. Milgramm is an accomplished executive with more than 25 years of experience in senior positions in the high-tech industry, with expertise in biometric technologies, authentication, encryption, and security systems. His experience also encompasses software development planning and execution of distributed strategic systems that position companies for success in implementation of emerging technologies to meet dynamic business demands.

Previously, Mr. Milgramm served as Senior Vice President at Marine Computers, where he managed a staff of 120 software and technical professionals and oversaw the development of large information systems for banks and the transportation industry.

Mr. Milgramm currently holds ten patents and patent applications specifically related to brain activity and biometric solutions, including a unique platform of independent biometric identification technology: the Multiplatform Independent Biometric Identification System.

Mr. Milgramm holds a Master of Computer Science and a Master in Economics, both from the St. Petersburg Institute of Technology.

Brett McDowell

Brett McDowell is a technology and policy evangelist for PayPal, driving increased adoption of information security standards and best practices across the Internet ecosystem. Brett has spent his career fostering collaborative development and global adoption of open technology and policy standards, primarily in the area of consumer privacy and security.

Prior to joining PayPal, he spent the past decade overseeing the development and promotion of several open standards, holding senior management positions with a variety of international organizations including Liberty Alliance Project, Open Mobile Alliance, VoiceXML Forum, IMS Global Learning Consortium, the SyncML Initiative, and most recently, serving as executive director of the Kantara Initiative where he managed the strategic direction of the organization and coordinated its liaison activities with numerous external industry groups, standards bodies and government agencies worldwide. Brett has played an integral part in the development of digital identity standards and best practices.

Over his tenure focused on digital identity, Brett has also been a speaker at several conferences & CXO venues including the RSA Security Conference, CTST Conference, FSTC BITS Summit, GTEC, The Research Board, the CSC CIO Study Tour and has represented his organizations as liaison to ITU-T, ISO, INCITS CS1, a variety of EU-funded Research Consortia, OASIS, W3C, ANSI IDSP & HITSP, ICTSB, OECD ITAC, among others.

Brett received a Bachelor of Science degree in physics from Alma College and a Lemelson Fellowship for Invention & Innovation at Hampshire College.

Andrew Nash

Andrew Nash is Senior Director of Identity Services at PayPal. He is a board member of the OpenID, Information Card and Kantara Foundations. Formerly he was CTO at Sonoa Systems and Reactivity working on XML and Web Services appliances. In 2006 he was recognized by InfoWorld as one of the "Top 25 Most Influential CTO's".

As Director of Technologies at RSA Security, Andrew worked on a wide range of identity systems. He is a known leader in PKI and Web-Services markets, has co-authored numerous Web Services security specifications and is author of a book on Public Key Infrastructure.

Mike Mulholand, Director, Fraud Solutions Strategy, Memento Inc.

In his thirty-year banking career, Mike has had management roles in bank operations and product management responsibilities in treasury services, deposits, fraud solutions, and compliance solutions. He has been involved in development and application of technology in a wide range of payments, corporate banking, and risk management projects. Throughout his career, he has had exposure to many technical and business aspects of banking. His experience has given him a perspective of business and technology issues in the banking industry from both a banker's and vendor's point of view.

Mike is currently an active member of the WEB/TEL workgroup of NACHA's Internet Council, and he has been a faculty member of the NACHA Payments Institute on the topic of ACH fraud risk. He has also been a keynote speaker on ACH fraud and other topics at major industry events. Mike is active in the Santa Fe Group: Vendor Council as the Steering Committee chair, a workgroup leader, or contributing author on white papers on ACH risk, internal fraud, and risk implications of payments system changes.

Mike holds an MBA from Capital University in Columbus, Ohio, and he has completed the course work for a master's degree in economic crime management at Utica College.

Mike served in the United States Marine Corps, where he achieved the rank of captain.

Randy Vanderhoof, Executive Director, Smart Card Alliance

Randy is the executive director of the Smart Card Alliance, a not-for-profit, multi-industry association of over one hundred and eighty member firms working to accelerate the widespread acceptance of smart card technology in North America and Latin America. He came to the Alliance in January 2002 and became the executive director in August 2002. During his tenure as the chief executive, he has directed the transformation of the organization from primarily a networking organization into a diverse, education-oriented, international, multi-industry organization that gathers industry stakeholders together to help stimulate the rapid adoption of all forms of smart cards (cards and other form factors) for electronic payments and digital security applications. In December 2008, Security named Randy to the list of the top twenty-five most influential people in the security industry.

Prior to joining the Smart Card Alliance, he was employed with IBM Global Smart Card Solutions, an international product group supporting IBM's smart card services to its global banking, health care, and government industry vertical teams. Previously, he served on the executive board for the Alliance as a corporate member from 1998 to 2001. From 2000 to 2001, he was vice president of business development with First Access, Inc., a developer of contactless smart card technology for network access security and authentication. From 1995 to 2000, he worked at Schlumberger (now Gemalto) as market segment manager, and Campus Solutions, supporting the development and marketing of smart card–based identification and payment systems.

Randy is a graduate of Saint Joseph's University in Philadelphia with a bachelor of science degree in management marketing. He received his MBA from Rider University in Lawrenceville, New Jersey.

Laura Mather, PhD, Founder and Vice President of Product Marketing, Silver Tail Systems

Laura is an expert in combating Internet fraud. She co-founded Silver Tail Systems, providing next-generation fraud prevention software in the fight against business logic abuse. As managing director of operational policy with the Anti-Phishing Working Group, she drives anti-fraud and anti-phishing policies to fight electronic crime. She also spent three years leading fraud prevention at eBay.

As the co-founder and CEO, Laura is a worldwide expert in combating

Internet fraud and a sought-after speaker, published author, and expert witness on the topic. She has spoken at IRS and FTC events in addition to many security conferences and events. She is also the managing director of operational policy for the Anti-Phishing Working Group where she drives Internet policy to fight electronic crimes of phishing, pharming, and spoofing. Prior to co-founding Silver Tail Systems with Mike, she spent three years in fraud prevention and anti-phishing at eBay, one of the brands most targeted by fraudsters on the Internet. Before eBay, she was a director of research and analysis for the online division of Encyclopedia Britannica and a research analyst for the National Security Agency (NSA). Laura holds a PhD in computer science and a bachelor of science degree in applied mathematics, both from the University of Colorado. Laura enjoys hiking and traveling.

Dr. Siva G. Narendra, Co-founder and CTO, Tyfone Inc

Siva is co-founder and CTO of Tyfone responsible for its product architecture, roadmap, and IP. Before his current responsibility, he was with Intel Laboratories specializing in energy and yield aware designs. He has authored over 60 technical papers in peer reviewed conferences and journals, and frequently lectures on technology forums. He also has over 100 issued/pending patents and holds 5 divisional recognition awards from Intel and an award in 2003 for having 19 issued patents in that year.

Siva is a frequent speaker at a wide range of forums including ones sponsored by academia and industry as well as organizations such as IEEE, FSTC, CTIA, SmartCard Alliance and FTC. He is a co-author and editor of the Leakage [Energy] in Nanometer CMOS Technologies book published by Springer. Siva is an Adjunct Faculty with the Departments of Electrical and Computer Engineering at Portland State University and Oregon State University. He is the Chair of Technology Directions sub-committee at the International Solid-State Circuit Conference and has been an active member of the Technical Program Committees of A-SSCC, and International Symposiums focusing on Low Power Design (ISLPED) and Quality Electronic Design (ISQED).

Siva has a Ph.D. degree in Electrical Engineering from Massachusetts Institute of Technology.

Craig Priess, Founder and Vice President of Products, Guardian Analytics

Craig directs Guardian Analytics' product strategy. In this role he ensures the company's products meet the ever-changing fraud prevention needs of financial institutions. Prior to founding Guardian Analytics, Craig spearheaded marketing efforts at Above All Software, a provider of integration technologies based on service-oriented architectures. Prior to Above All Software, he held product marketing and product management roles with several early stage enterprise software companies. Craig also spent five years each at CRM pioneer The Vantive Corporation and Westinghouse Electric Corporation. He received a BS in Industrial Engineering & Operations Research from UC Berkeley and an MBA from the University of Baltimore.

Scott West, Product Manager, FIS Image

Scott joined FIS in November of 2001 after spending several years in a variety of positions at Security National Bank / Arvest Bank. Scott has over 16 years experience in banking and financial software, and has worked in all areas of banking including the credit, accounting, compliance, loan review, and back office / teller departments. In his current role Scott is responsible for providing strategic product marketing direction for the FIS Image fraud prevention solutions. Scott is a sought after speaker and panelist at payments industry events for FIS.

Scott holds a Bachelor's Degree in Economics from University of Oklahoma.

Steven Schaeffer, FIS

Steven Schaeffer has been in the banking industry for 20+ years. He has held Liability and Risk Management positions with Bank of America and General Electric with responsibilities spanning fraud management and prevention, claims management, Texas retail operations, Investigation teams and collections management. In the product management discipline Steven developed and managed fraud solutions for Carreker, Fiserv, and FIS. He is a member of CAMS, NACHA, and Pragmatic Marketing certified.

Kevin Roper, SVP & General Manager, FIS Image and Item Processing Solutions Division

Kevin is an experienced technology executive with a successful history of running small to large software and services businesses specializing in the financial services, insurance, utilities, and government industries. Prior to joining FIS Kevin held executive management positions with DSL Roper Associates, InSystems Inc., a subsidiary of Standard Register, and BancTec, Inc.

Kevin is a graduate of Dennison University and received an MBA in finance and accounting from the SMU Cox School of Business.

Luther Martin, Chief Security Architect, Voltage Security, Inc

Luther Martin is the Chief Security Architect at Voltage Security, Inc., a vendor of encryption technology and products. He began his career in information security at the National Security Agency, where he graduated from the NSA's Cryptologic Mathematician Program in 1991, and eventually became the Technical Director of the NSA's Engineering and Physical Sciences Security Division.

After leaving the NSA, he has worked at both security consulting and product companies. Notable accomplishments during this period include creating the security code review for consulting firm Ernst & Young, running the first commercial security code review projects, and creating the public-key infrastructure technology that was used in the US Postal Service's PC Postage program.

He has given invited talks on the topic of information security at the Naval Postgraduate School, the National Security Agency, the Department of Homeland Security, the National Institute for Standards and Technology and the Office of the Director of National Intelligence's Summer Hard Problem Program, as well as at leading commercial information security conferences. He is the author of the book *Introduction to Identity-based Encryption*, contributions to five other books and over 100 articles on the topics of information security and risk management.

He is also the author of three Internet Engineering Task Force security standards (RFC 5091, RFC 5408, RFC 5409), is the Technical Editor of the IEEE P1363.3 Standard for Identity-based Public-key Cryptography Using Pairings, and is active in the Accredited Standards Committee X9F working groups that define the information security standards used in the US financial services industry.

His daily thoughts on information security can be found at http://superconductor.voltage.com/.

Dena Hamilton, Norkom Technologies

Dena Hamilton is responsible for the strategic direction of Norkom's Multi-Channel Payment Fraud solutions. With more than 20 years' experience working in financial crime, Dena joined Norkom in 2010 having spent 14 years in the payment engine software industry, successfully leading the build and launch of fraud detection solutions focused on card, merchant, AML and multi-channel fraud transaction monitoring. Prior to this, she spent 15 years at Bank One, Columbus NA and Banc One Financial Card Services, working within the retail, wholesale and third-party card processing divisions. Dena served in numerous capacities, spending the last five years as a Senior Business Analyst, specializing in card authorizations, Visa and MasterCard requirements with a concentrated focus in fraud detection for broker processing and credit/debit card lines of business.

Peter G. Tapling, President and CEO, Authentify Inc

Peter Tapling co-founded Authentify in 1999 and has held the position of President and CEO ever since. Tapling joined Authentify from Aurigin Systems (acquired by MicroPatent), and prior to that was Vice President of Strategic Development for NetDox and President of IDMetrix, a NetDox subsidiary. Tapling previously held senior management positions at startups in the information security and application development markets. He brings a wealth of industry and management experience having had responsibility, at various times, for sales, marketing, business development, finance and technical services. Tapling has concentrated his efforts on early-stage companies, both as a principal and advisor.

Tapling is an executive director of the Illinois Information Technology Association; a member of the Dean's Advisory Board of the College of Applied Sciences and Technology at Illinois State University; and acts as a mentor to entrepreneurs and an advisor to a collection of small enterprises. He is a frequent speaker at industry forums. Tapling earned a B.S. degree in Applied Computer Science from Illinois State University.

Knud Balslev, VP of Business Development, FonWallet Transaction Solutions Inc

Knud has over 15 years of experience in business development and alliance management most recently, as Director of Global Alliances with IdenTrust, a leader in digital identities used by banks and large enterprises to secure payments. Knud worked in a variety of business development and management positions at HP/Compaq/DEC, focusing on strategic alliances primarily in the finance, telecom and high availability computing segments. He developed business with global solution partners and enabled revenue growth from pre-paid and billing solutions for mobile telecom operators, to keep up with the phenomenal growth period in the early 2000s. Knud has extensive international experience gained from working and living in Europe and the U.S. His language skills include English, Danish, French, & German and are used to facilitate engagement with partners and customers globally. Knud has a B.Sc. degree in Electrical Engineering from the Technical University of Copenhagen, Denmark.

Clifford Stanford, Assistant Vice President, Bank Supervision and Regulation Division, Federal Reserve Bank of Atlanta

Cliff is an assistant vice president in the bank supervision and regulation division at the Federal Reserve Bank of Atlanta, where he is responsible for its banking applications and enforcement functions. Prior to assuming his current role in 2010, Cliff served as assistant vice president and founding director of the Retail Payments Risk Forum at the Federal Reserve Bank of Atlanta, where he worked in collaboration with industry participants, regulators, and law enforcement to identify, understand, and mitigate emerging risks in electronic payments systems. He also served as assistant vice president in the human resources department of the Federal Reserve Bank of Atlanta from 2006 to 2008, where was responsible for managing day-to-day human resources operations and assisting with the strategic direction of the bank's human resources function.

A native of Atlanta, Cliff joined the bank in 1996 as assistant counsel in the legal department, where he rose to assistant general counsel by 2004. In his legal role, he led the Federal Reserve system's intellectual property protection efforts and was a key bank resource in numerous legal areas, including contracts, banking regulation, employment law, ethics, payments law, and litigation.

Cliff earned a juris doctorate from Georgia State University in 1995 and a bachelor's degree in history from Emory University in 1992. He has been a member of the State Bar of Georgia since 1995. He is a member of the board of directors of St. Jude's Recovery Center and a past president of the alumni association for Georgia State University's College of Law.

SPONSORING/CONTRIBUTING ORGANIZATION BRIEFS

FS-ISAC

FS-ISAC shares critical, authoritative information across a range of industry players instantly.

Launched in 1999, FS-ISAC was established by the financial services sector in response to the Presidential Directive 63 in 1998. That directive, later updated by Homeland Security Presidential Directive 7 in 2003, mandated that the public and private sectors share information about physical and cyber security threats and vulnerabilities to help protect the American critical infrastructure.

Constantly gathering reliable and timely information from financial services providers; commercial security firms; federal, state, and local government agencies; law enforcement; and other trusted resources, the FS-ISAC is now uniquely positioned to quickly disseminate physical and cyber threat alerts and other critical information to your organization. This information includes analysis and recommended solutions from leading industry experts.

The FS-ISAC provides rapid and trusted protection for our companies, our industry, and our country. Bad news travels fast. When it comes to cyber security threats against financial services firms, that adage has never been more accurate. Now, thanks to the FS-ISAC, help is arriving just as quickly.

The recent successful completion of our Critical Infrastructure Notification System (CINS) allows the FS-ISAC to speed security alerts to multiple recipients near-simultaneously while providing for user authentication and delivery confirmation. The FS-ISAC also provides an anonymous information-sharing capability across the entire financial services industry. Upon receiving a submission, industry experts verify and analyze the threat and identify any recommended solutions before alerting FS-ISAC members. This assures that member firms receive the latest tried-and-true procedures and best practices for guarding against known and emerging security threats.

Joining the FS-ISAC is one of the best ways financial services firms can do their part to protect our industry and its vital role in the American critical infrastructure. To that end, FS-ISAC membership is recommended by the United States Department of the Treasury, the Office of the Comptroller of Currency, the Department of Homeland Security (DHS), the United States Secret Service, and the Financial Services Sector Coordinating Council. In fact, both Treasury and DHS rely on the FS-ISAC to disseminate critical information to the financial services sector in times of crisis.

Armor Safe Technologies

Armor Safe Technologies specializes in the development, deployment, and servicing of the industry's most innovative cash management systems. Our safes validate, count, and secure cash in cassettes ready for delivery to your bank, establishing an effective closed-loop solution for many of your toughest challenges: loss prevention, employee accountability, and financial transparency.

We customize our safes to meet your needs and create a cash management solution that cost-effectively protects your assets. As the industry leader in innovation, we are constantly developing and delivering new technologies to ensure that, together, we'll overcome your current and future cash management challenges.

Much more than a safe, our products reduce labor costs, generate detailed reports, and provide seamless accounting from the cash register to the bank with the utmost security every step of the way. That's the power of smart technology.

We significantly improve your operational efficiency by integrating seamlessly into your business. You'll save time and money, and your investment will begin paying for itself on day one because fewer people will be handling your cash.

With Armor Safe Technologies working hard for your money, you can spend more time on what matters most, serving your customers, developing your people, and growing your business. These big jobs are made easier with the improved productivity, accountability, and transparency that an Armor safe will provide.

Armor Safe Technologies has established strategic partnerships with the world's leading armored car carriers, and every Armor safe features world-renowned components like MEI's bill validator to provide the highest level of cash security.

Orbograph

Orbograph is a leading provider of recognition-centric software and services for the check processing and forms processing markets. Orbograph's innovative technologies are in use in over one thousand financial institutions and service bureaus, processing billions of checks and forms annually. Through check processing automation, fraud prevention, data mining for marketing, and forms processing automation solutions, Orbograph enables clients to envision more for their organization by reducing costs, managing risk, and driving revenue growth while ensuring that achieving more is a reality.

The 41st Parameter

As leaders in fraud intervention, 41st Parameter's innovative solutions help you protect your customers and your brand, reduce fraud losses, and make the Internet a safer place to conduct business. Through a combination of best practices, leading technology, and human interaction, our innovative solutions provide an unprecedented level of Internet security, decrease the anonymity of the Internet, and help you gain valuable insight into every online transaction and customer interaction. We make the process of preventing and detecting Internet fraud easier and more effective, reducing both expenses and potential losses.

41st Parameter provides solutions for detecting and preventing fraud across multiple channels for the world's most valued and recognizable brands. Leading financial institutions, e-commerce companies, and travel services businesses rely on 41st Parameter's technology to protect them from cyber crime threats including card not present fraud, new account origination fraud, phishing and account compromise, credit bust outs, and fraud ring attacks. Founded in 2004, 41st Parameter makes the process of detecting and preventing fraud easier and more effective, reducing both expenses and potential losses. As a leading Web fraud detection innovator, the company supplies industry-proven solutions that integrate advanced device identification with comprehensive risk management capabilities.

IdentaZone, Inc

IdentaZone, Inc specializes in innovative security technologies and products that utilize all forms of biometric authentication to provide enterprise-wide platform-independent solutions for infrastructure, data and communications protection. Technologies developed and implemented by the company address the pressing needs of the marketplace for integrated customizable security and identity management solutions that allow concurrent use of multiple biometric technologies and devices. Co-Founder and Vice President/CTO Michael Milgramm, currently own's 10 patents and patent applications specifically related to biometric solutions.

Headquartered in New York, IdentaZone, Inc specializes in providing innovative and unique biometric security software and solutions. IdentaZone has been developing and offering unique complete biometric solutions to secure key enterprise and individual user data assets, content, and privacy by utilizing the latest multi-vendor advancements in biometric technologies.

IdentaZone believes that key elements of corporate security and personal, which include strong authentication (identity verification), authorization, access control, confidentiality, integrity and privacy, can be attained by deploying and effectively managing a platform independent biometric security infrastructure that emphasizes both enterprise-level and individual user features. IdentaZone also believes that strong and modular underlying technology platforms can be translated both into horizontal and industry-specific products. Its mission has been to create future-proof technologies and products that seamlessly blend platform-independent biometric-based identity verification with existing and future security systems, while essentially being transparent to the end-users.

Memento

Memento, Inc. is a recognized leader in enterprise fraud management. Memento Security, the company's award-winning solution, is an innovative platform for monitoring, detecting, and investigating fraud and inappropriate activities by a wide range of fraudsters from trusted insiders to criminal outsiders. Used by the world's largest and most influential financial institutions, Memento solutions are business-focused, easy to use, and quick to implement. By detecting inappropriate activities early and precisely, Memento gives enterprises the information they need to prevent loss, protect revenue, and mitigate risk.

Memento was founded in 2003 to solve two of the most critical unsolved problems faced by financial services enterprises: fighting fraud and managing compliance. From the start, Memento's leaders recognized that the traditional ways of attempting to address these complex, dynamic issues were ineffective, inflexible, and overly complicated. They saw an opportunity waiting for the right solution.

Our team of technologists and industry veterans created Memento Security from the ground up to take a fundamentally different approach, one that drew upon proprietary indexing, advanced fraud-scenario modeling, and monitoring techniques to zero in on the telltale events and patterns that include fraud and compliance issues.

As the company expanded, we focused on applying our solution and unique approach to the wide-ranging challenges of fraud and compliance, including check fraud, employee fraud, bust-out fraud, health-care fraud, regulatory issues, and more. In each case, we provide a solution that is more accurate, flexible, faster, and better than traditional approaches. And we work closely with our customers to meet the ever-changing challenges they face.

Since its founding, the company has grown steadily and quickly, attracting a loyal base of customers, including credit unions, community banks, larger banks across North America and Europe, and health-care institutions. Though the company has grown, our focus remains the same, fighting fraud and managing compliance.

The Smart Card Alliance

The Smart Card Alliance is a not-for-profit, multi-industry association working to stimulate the understanding, adoption, use, and widespread application of smart card technology. Through specific projects such as education programs, market research, advocacy, industry relations, and open forums, the Alliance keeps its members connected to industry leaders and innovative thought. The Alliance is the single industry voice for smart cards, leading industry discussion on the impact and value of smart cards in the United States and Latin America.

The Smart Card Alliance membership includes over one hundred and eighty organizations that are leading companies in the financial services, computer, telecommunications, technology, health care, retail, security, and transportation industries, as well as a number of government agencies. The Alliance brings together leading users and technologists from both the public and private sectors. Membership is open to any organization focusing resources based on the smart card technology.

Smart Card Alliance Priorities

- Serve as an educational resource to its members and the industry on emerging smart card adoption issues
- Provide a forum for cutting-edge discussions and group projects that positively influence the implementation of smart card technology
- Engage industry to influence standards that are relevant to smart card adoption and implementation
- Maintain a voice in public policy that affects smart card adoption and implementation

Smart Card Alliance Activities

Industry and Technology Councils. To accomplish its goals, the Alliance has member-driven industry and technology councils that explore issues and define requirements in key markets or technology areas. Groups collaborate on specific deliverables, including reports, briefings, and educational material.

Conferences. The Smart Card Alliance holds three conferences per year. These events are designed to provide information to attendees that will assist them in the development and implementation of smart card initiatives.

Professional Development and Certification. The Smart Card Alliance launched a bold initiative in 2009 to provide world-leading smart card training and educational resources for industry professionals interested in furthering their knowledge and advancing their careers. The result was the first official certification program for smart card professionals (CSCIP) along with a personal membership program providing comprehensive educational resources and social networking services, the Leadership, Education, and Advancement Program (LEAP).

Industry Networking. The more than 1,350 mostly mid- to senior-level industry professionals participating in Smart Card Alliance activities represent engineering, marketing, business development, and sales for major supplier, integration, and issuing organizations, creating a rich business community that fosters valuable networking opportunities.

Silver Tail Systems

Silver Tail Systems provides third-generation fraud prevention to protect against business logic abuse, the abuse of legitimate Web pages to perpetrate fraud. Silver Tail products use real-time behavior analysis to detect and alert on known threats and new behaviors like Man-in-the-Browser and Zeus, and then enable the fraud and security analysts to disrupt these attacks in real time. Founded by fraud prevention experts from eBay and PayPal, Silver Tail significantly reduces online fraud losses, protects Web sites, and increases customer trust.

Hackers are no longer high school kids trying to one-up their friends or criminals trying to just break into sites. Instead, today's sophisticated hacker is organized crime, strategically targeting Web sites, stealing billions of dollars from companies and their customers. Vendors providing Web application security and intrusion prevention have forced hackers to become much more innovative in their means of attacking Web sites. These hackers now target the legitimate business logic of Web sites to perpetrate their fraud, including hijack threats, automated programs for password guessing, mass registration of accounts to game incentive programs, scraping customer data off the Web site to perpetrate identity theft, and many others. Silver Tail is using the deep domain expertise of its team to provide software that combats business logic abuse in real time. Silver Tail provides a new generation of fraud prevention:

- **Behavioral analysis.** Silver Tail provides proactive identification of new and suspicious behavior on a Web site or event. Web sites no longer have to rely on their customers to report problems. Silver Tail detects the behavior in real time and immediately sends notifications and alerts.
- **Investigation tools.** Silver Tail provides easy and efficient tools for investigating exploits and suspicious behavior. No more culling through Web logs to determine how bad actors are perpetrating their fraud.
- **Immediate response.** Business owners can immediately change business logic flows for the bad actors without impacting good users in real time and without requiring engineering resources.

A team of fraud prevention experts who built anti-fraud and anti-phishing tools at eBay and PayPal founded Silver Tail. Through their experience and proprietary algorithms, they have built a system that is scalable, minimizes false positive rates, and is extremely flexible to adapt to changing attack vectors. Silver Tail's recent work with several popular Web sites has found that as much as 50 percent of traffic can be robotic with a substantial amount of live exploits at any point in time. Most of this had been completely undetected by the sites. Silver Tail forensics took minutes to discover the exploits, saving these companies weeks of analysis. Silver Tail mitigation helps to divert and block the bad behavior in real time, saving the cost of resources to rewrite pages.

Tyfone, Inc

Tyfone is a neutral infrastructure enabler for cloud computing based mobile services. Tyfone enables the next wave of secure-element-neutral mobile apps that are secure enough to store your Driver's License, Health Records, Passport, Debit, Pre-paid and Credit Cards.

Tyfone's u4ia® platform and its companion SideTap™ card is the world's first patented memory card-based mobile payments solution with integrated secure element, OTA controller and miniature contactless coil for mobile NFC payments. The technology operates in any standard memory card slot and is rapidly gaining market acceptance as a single-strategy approach to mobile contactless payments for any mobile phone. Tyfone and its partners enable a suite of services including Mobile Banking, Mobile Identity Management, Mobile Remote Payments, Mobile Retail Services and Mobile Contactless Payments.

Guardian Analytics

Based in Los Altos, CA, Guardian Analytics helps financial institutions of all sizes protect their customers and their reputations by proactively detecting the online account takeover that leads to ACH, wire, call center and other forms of fraud. Guardian Analytics leverages its deep technical knowledge connecting data analytics, the online domain, and fraud expertise. Our FraudMAP solution takes a progressive approach to fraud prevention and uses behavioral analytics to detect fraudulent account activity in retail and business accounts. Founded in 2005, the company is privately held with venture funding from Foundation Capital and Sutter Hill Ventures.

FIS

FIS is the world's top-ranked technology provider to the banking industry. With more than Thirty-thousand experts serving 14,000 clients in one hundred countries, FIS delivers the most comprehensive range of solutions for the broadest range of financial markets, all with a singular focus of helping clients succeed. Every FIS solution has the strength you need for profitability today and the power to help you manage whatever comes next.

FIS is part of the S&P 500. FIS has also been named the number-one overall financial technology provider in the world by *American Banker* and *Financial Insights* (FinTech 100).

Voltage Security, Inc

Voltage Security helps organizations with sensitive customer information e.g. cardholder data to protect that information wherever it goes – databases, applications, POS devices, partners, customers and payment processors – using end-to-end encryption, tokenization and masking. Voltage solutions are rapidly gaining adoption and are already in use by 3 of the top 5 US payment processors (Heartland, Fifth Third Processing Solutions and Elavon), POS device manufacturers as well as merchants, insurance companies, telecommunication companies and other large financial services companies. Bank Technology News recently declared Voltage Security to be one of its top innovators for 2010, for its breakthrough approaches to protecting and transmitting data securely with innovative cryptography and simplified key management. In addition to protecting cardholder data, Voltage provides solutions for protecting emails, files and other types of structured and unstructured data. In fact, some of the largest companies in the world rely on Voltage security solutions to protect data end-to-end for their compliance and security needs – internally and with customers and partners.

Norkom Technologies

Established in 1998, Norkom Technologies (AIM: NORK.L, IEX: NORK. IE) enables financial organisations to take intelligent action, control defences, and evolve strategies against fraud, money laundering, and other types of financial crime. By combining a unique investigative technology platform with deep domain expertise, Norkom has established a solid track record of reducing financial losses, protecting users' reputations, improving operational efficiencies, and lowering the cost of information technology. Norkom serves clients in over 100 countries across four continents including HSBC, Banco Santander, Bank of Montreal, Credit Agricole, DnB NOR, Dubai Islamic Bank and Standard Chartered Bank.

Authentify, Inc

Founded in 1999, Authentify, Inc. provides automated authentication services for many of the largest online business enterprises operating today. The Authentify service enables organizations to quickly and cost-effectively perform real-time, multi-factor user authentication during an Internet session. By leveraging the familiarity of the telephone networks, Authentify delivers an effective multi-factor authentication process that is practical for business and easy for end users.

Authentify's patented technology employs a message-based architecture to seamlessly integrate with existing online processes developed for e-business, secure information access, or the distribution of security credentials. By synchronizing a user's web session with an automated telephone call, Authentify makes undeniable contact with the person behind the computer while capturing transaction details for audit purposes.

Authentify provides end users with an intuitive authentication process that does not require additional software or training on the user's behalf. With its multi-language compatibility using landline or mobile phones, Authentify's service offers a truly portable authentication solution with worldwide reach.

FonWallet Transaction Solutions, Inc

FonWallet Transaction Solutions, Inc. provides m-based transaction solutions for the credit card, carrier and banking industries. Founded in 2006, the FonWallet solution is built to drive value, security and benefits to the entire transaction chain. More information about FonWallet is available at www.fonwallet.com.